Edward

THE PRESENCE OF CHRIST IN THE HOLY EUCHARIST

A

SERMON

PREACHED BEFORE THE UNIVERSITY

IN THE CATHEDRAL CHURCH

IN OXFORD

ON THE SECOND SUNDAY AFTER

Elibron Classics
www.elibron.com

Elibron Classics series.

© 2005 Adamant Media Corporation.

ISBN 1-4021-6817-9 (paperback)
ISBN 1-4212-8261-5 (hardcover)

This Elibron Classics Replica Edition is an unabridged facsimile
of the edition published in 1895 by J. H. Parker, Oxford; Francis
& John Rivington, London.

THE PRESENCE OF CHRIST IN THE HOLY EUCHARIST.

A

SERMON,

PREACHED BEFORE THE UNIVERSITY,

IN THE CATHEDRAL CHURCH OF CHRIST,

In Oxford,

ON THE SECOND SUNDAY AFTER EPIPHANY, 1853.

BY THE REV.

E. B. PUSEY, D.D.

REGIUS PROFESSOR OF HEBREW ; CANON OF CHRIST CHURCH ;
LATE FELLOW OF ORIEL COLLEGE.

Christ is my Food.
S. AMBROSE.

PRINTED FOR
JOHN HENRY PARKER, OXFORD, & 377, STRAND, LONDON :
AND
FRANCIS & JOHN RIVINGTON,
ST. PAUL'S CHURCH YARD, AND WATERLOO PLACE, LONDON.
MDCCCLIII.

LONDON:

GILBERT AND RIVINGTON, PRINTERS,

ST. JOHN'S SQUARE.

PREFACE.

My former Sermon,—"The Holy Eucharist a comfort to the Penitent,"—was misunderstood by some, because it was not controversial. My object in it was not to *teach* the doctrine of the Holy Eucharist, but rather, assuming the doctrine of the Church of England to be identical (as I believe it to be) with that of the Fathers, to present that doctrine in one aspect as "a comfort to the penitent." To this end I dwelt, not on the doctrine of the Real Presence in itself, nor even on the mode in which "the Body and Blood of Christ are verily and indeed taken and received by the faithful in the Lord's Supper," but on the exceeding greatness of the Gift which is thus conveyed to the soul. I wished to impress on the souls of my hearers, the actualness and closeness of the union of man's soul with its Redeemer, and in Him with God, wrought through that sacrament. I wished to aid to lift up the hearts of true peni-

tents, by showing them what stores of Mercy and
Divine love, and nearness to God in Christ, were yet
open to them.

One object alone, or at least above all others, I
had in view in the whole course of Sermons, of
which this Sermon was a part, "the comfort of the
penitent." I wished to set forth to the weary and
broken-hearted, the comforts in store for those who
in truth, not in word, were "grieved and wearied
with the burden of their sins." To the penitent
the special comfort of the Holy Eucharist is, that it
is the Body and Blood of his Redeemer; "that his
sinful body is made clean by His Body, and his soul
washed through His most Precious Blood." This
being so clearly embodied in the prayers of our
Church, it never even occurred to me, until after
the Sermon was preached, that any grave question
could be raised upon it. I was prepared for the
sort of objection which, for ten years, had been raised
on the doctrine of Baptism, and on that ground, and
in order (if it might be) to bring home to men's
minds the unseemliness of angry and irreverent
disputing on this, which our Saviour left "as the
pledges of His love to our great and endless comfort," I made the appeal in the outset of my
Sermon [1]. I suspected nothing, and so I scarcely

---

[1] The Holy Eucharist a Comfort to the Penitent, p. 3.

guarded any thing. I thought that it must be enough to state generally that I did, without inquiring or defining, believe that we received at once elements of this world and His very Body and Blood. I said, "We [2], if we are wise, shall never ask, *how* they can be elements of this world, and yet His very Body and Blood." Having said this, I imagined that the rest of my Sermon would be understood in the same sense. It never even came into my mind to apprehend, that language of the Fathers, which simply expresses the reality of the Gift, could be thought to contradict the Church of England, which asserts the same reality.

My object throughout that Sermon was to show how, through the Holy Eucharist, we have life from our living and loving Lord Himself, re-creation in Him, and the earnest of endless joy and bliss in Him. To this end, I selected passages from the Fathers which spoke most fervently of the closeness of the union with our Lord, which He vouchsafes thereby to bestow upon us. I wished altogether to avoid controversy, and not to risk distracting men's minds from the one object which I desired to bring before them, the greatness of our loving Saviour's gift to *them*, and His unspeakable goodness. Men's minds so easily go off upon controversy, that I thought it right

[2] Ib. p. 7.

to avoid what would raise it.   In quoting, then, from
the Fathers, I *did* purposely abstain from citing passages which might bear one way or the other upon
modern controversy.   I alluded neither to those passages which spoke of the outward elements as figures
or symbols, nor yet to the opposite class which might
be supposed, at first sight, to favour a belief of a
physical change.   Had I been writing a treatise on
the Holy Eucharist, and referred to the Fathers, it
would, of course, have been necessary expressly to
consider them.   This could not be done in a Sermon,
and, in whatever degree it had been attempted, it
would have changed the subject of the Sermon from
that which I had in view.   It may then help to save
hard judgment in another case, to notice that a
writer in the "Dublin Review," while allowing that
my Sermon was a fair representation of the teaching of the Fathers, up to a certain point (*i.e.* as he
thought, as far as our Articles permitted), charged
me with unfairness, for omitting what, as he thought,
went beyond it.   I simply did not quote what did
not bear upon my immediate subject, and might
have thrown the mind into a controversial frame,
instead of that which I wished to cherish, one loving,
grateful, and devotional.

The doctrine of the present Sermon is the same
as that in the former.   But in this Sermon I have

dwelt on the doctrine of the Holy Eucharist in itself; and have, therefore, of necessity, spoken more distinctly on the objective Presence of our Lord therein; and, on the other hand, I have stated grounds why I believe, with the Church of England, that this real and objective Presence does not involve any physical change in the natural elements, which are the veils and channels of our Lord's Unseen Presence.

It is, I believe, the explanation of the former Sermon which, had opportunity been allowed, I should have given ten years ago.

The dimensions of a sermon can only present a bare outline of the argument on a subject. I have, on account of the importance of the subject, and with the memory of my former condemnation, entered more into details than I should have otherwise thought advisable in the pulpit. The notes will indicate what I hope, if God will, to fill out in an Appendix.

In the mean while, I trust that it may, by God's grace, suggest some earnest and reverent thoughts to those, for whose souls' sake it was preached.

CHRIST CHURCH,
Easter, 1853.

A

SERMON,

&c.

---

1 Corinthians x. 16.

" The cup of blessing which we bless, is it not the communion
of the blood of Christ? The bread which we break, is it not
the communion of the body of Christ?"

THE Holy Eucharist is plainly the closest union of
man with God. Through the Incarnation God took
our nature, took the Manhood into God. But although we had that unspeakable nearness to Himself, in that the Co-eternal Son, God *of* God, and
God *with* God, took not the nature of Angels, but
took the Manhood into God; this was a gift to our
whole race. It was a gift which, by its very nature,
must overflow to us individually; yet still it required
a further act of God's condescension fully to apply
it to each one of us. God the Word became Flesh.
Yet hereby He was in His Human Nature one *with*
us; we were not, as yet, made " one with Him."

We belonged to Him as His creatures. Unutterable was the love whereby, when man was fallen,

He took part of all our miseries, except our sins, and the sinfulness of our nature; and these, which He could not take *to* Himself, He took *on* Himself: what *we* could not bear, He bare *for* us. But although we were thereby reconciled to God, as His creatures, we were not yet united to Him individually. We could not be united to Him, save by His communicating Himself to us. This He willed to do by indwelling in us through His Spirit; by making us, through the Sacrament of Baptism, members of His Son; by giving us, through the Holy Eucharist, not in any carnal way, but really and spiritually, the Flesh and Blood of the Incarnate Son, whereby "He dwelleth in us, and we in Him; He is one with us, and we with Him." Through these, He imparteth to us the life which He Himself is. He, the Life of the world, maketh those alive, in whom He is. This is the comfort of the penitent, the joy of the faithful, the Paradise of the holy, the Heaven of those whose conversation is in Heaven, the purity of those who long to be partakers of His holiness, the strengthening of man's heart, the renewal of the inward man, the fervour of Divine love, spiritual peace, kindled hope, assured faith, burning thankfulness,—that our Lord Jesus Christ, not in figure, but in reality, although a spiritual reality, does give Himself to us, does come to be in us.

But nearness to God has also an awful aspect. " Our God is a consuming fire." Your consciences, my younger brethren, can best tell you whether your souls are arrayed in the wedding-garment which Christ gives, and which Christ requires in those who would approach to His Heavenly Feast, the wedding-garment of faith and love unfeigned, an upright and holy conversation, cleansed and made pure by the Blood of Christ; or whether, "grieving the Spirit of God, whereby ye were sealed," and " not led by the Spirit of God," ye are now (God forbid that ye should remain so) "none of His." I speak not now of the present, but of the past. Ye yourselves best know, how far ye differ from that past. But no one at any time can have known in any great degree, what were the habits of a large portion of the young in this place, or even the very outward fact, how, when man required it, almost all received the Holy Communion; how few, when God only called, and the young were left to their own consciences,—none can have observed this, without greatly fearing, that if too few are present in the one case, too many are present in the other.

The Church requires as conditions; repentance, faith, charity, a loving memory of the Passion of our Lord, and a stedfast purpose to lead a new life. This you are to ascertain for yourselves, by examining yourselves. God bids you by St. Paul; He exhorts you by the Church; " search and examine your own consciences, and that not lightly and after the manner of dissemblers with God, but so that ye may come holy and clean to such a Heavenly Feast."

Would that one were not compelled to think that many sought rather to forget themselves, than to examine themselves; to hide themselves from themselves; to put away their sins for a day or two, in order to resume them as before; as though the wedding-garment which God requires, might be laid aside, as soon as the Feast was over; or as if this unwilling abstinence of a few days from some besetting sin were the clothing of "the new man, which after God is created in righteousness and true holiness."

I would then, once more, my younger brethren, set before you the doctrine of the Holy Eucharist on both sides. And this, both because some, looking for too much clearness in their intellectual conception of Divine mysteries, are tempted to undue speculation in defining the mode of the Sacred Presence of our Lord; and others, practically, can hardly be thought to believe any real Presence at all; else they would not approach, as they do, so unrepenting and so careless.

It *is* a temptation, to require too precise theories, to desire to be able to state clearly to the understanding, that which is beyond all understanding. Thus, it is a very common, although untrue [1], plea

---

[1] It is held as a truth of faith by Roman divines too, that no one who does not die in a state of grace can go to heaven, and that after this life there is no obtaining of greater grace. The Roman doctrine of Purgatory is simply, that temporal punishment for sin is there endured, in the proportion required by Divine

for the doctrine of Purgatory, that it seems to explain how, those many who pass from this life in a very imperfect state, apparently unfit for Heaven, may yet be saved. Again, one and the same mind will vacillate between the most stringent statements of the Unity of the Church, and the most latitudinarian, as being, severally, clear to the understanding. Again, people think that unity would be best secured, if there were one visible head of the Church; that the analogy of a kingdom would best be maintained by a visible King; and so, they argue as if unity were not enough provided for, as our Lord left His Church. Others, again, have imagined a conditional fore-knowledge, in lieu of God's Omniscience, or a predestination to eternal woe, as evading, in opposite ways, the inextricable difficulty of admitting at once both man's free agency and the absolute knowledge of the All-wise God.

And so, as to the Holy Eucharist, men *can* conceive that the elements after consecration are only what they seem and what they were before, not the vehicle of an Unseen Presence; or, again, they *can* imagine that they are nothing but an outward show, and that the Body of Christ alone is present; they can forget either the Unseen Presence or the visible

Justice, but without any change in the soul, such as in this life is wrought by the Grace of God, amid the patient endurance of suffering for the love of God, or in penitential sorrow. I instanced this, because I have known persons desirous to believe the doctrine, as giving them better hope of being saved.

form, but they have difficulty in receiving the thought which the Church of England suggests in her words[2]: "of the due receiving of the blessed Body and Blood of our Saviour Christ *under* the form of bread and wine;" that the sacramental bread and wine "remain still in their very natural substances;" and yet that under these poor outward forms, "His creatures of bread and wine," "the faithful verily and indeed take and receive the Body and Blood of Christ."

And yet Holy Scripture, taken in its plainest meaning, affirms both that the outward elements remain, and still that there is the real Presence of the Body of Christ. And I may, in the outset, say, that when the Articles reject Transubstantiation, they themselves explain what they mean to reject, —a doctrine which "is repugnant to the plain words of Holy Scripture," *i.e.* those words in which our Lord and St. Paul speak of the natural substances as remaining. The Articles call it also "a doctrine which overthroweth the nature of a Sacrament," in that the outward and visible part is supposed to have no real subsistence. They except against no

---

[2] "Hereafter shall follow sermons of fasting, praying, alms-deeds, of the Nativity, Passion, Resurrection, and Ascension of our Saviour Christ, *of the due receiving of His Blessed Body and Blood under the form of bread and wine* : against idleness, against gluttony and drunkenness, against covetousness, against envy, ire, and malice, with many other matters, as well fruitful as necessary to the edifying of Christian people, and the edifying of godly living. Amen."—*End of first Book of Homilies.*

statement which does not imply that the natural substances cease to be.

To remove, in the outset, a misconstruction likely to occur. It will be said, " If the Church of England teaches that the consecrated elements remain in their very natural substances, and yet that the Body and Blood of Christ are present under those outward forms of bread and wine, then we are pledged to what is called Consubstantiation." This is altogether a mistake. The very term Consubstantiation is a mere term of reproach used against the Lutherans by those who denied any Sacred Presence at all [3]. To say that our Lord's Body was "consubstantiated" with the bread, would be the blasphemy of saying that It was united with the bread into one common substance.

In the indivisible Unity of God, we adore the Consubstantial Word which is the Son. Our Blessed Lord in His Divine Nature is Consubstantial with the Father; in His Human Nature, Consubstantial with us, as we confess in the Creed: " God, of the Substance of the Father, Begotten before the world, and Man, of the Substance of His Mother, Born in the world." His Body is Consubstantial with ours, of one common substance. Consubstantiation or Impanation [4] would be but physical explanations of

---

[3] See Gerhard de S. Cœna, § 104. Buddeus (de S. Cœna, § 27, in Miscell. S. ii. 84) quotes Hospinian, Prol. Conc. Disc. p. 6.

[4] "Consubstantiation " would be the union of two substances

the mystery of the Holy Eucharist. Such doctrines are said to have been held by one or two in the middle ages [5]. They are expressly denied by the Lutherans [6] to whom they are imputed, and are taught in none of their books. The strongest statement of the earliest Confession of Augsburg [7]—" Of the Supper of the Lord, it is taught that the very Body and Blood of Christ are verily present in the Lord's Supper, under the form of bread and wine, and are distributed, and taken in it,"—like that of our homilies, offers no physical explanation, but simply expresses the real unseen sacramental Presence under the outward visible form.

To receive literally, then, those words of our Lord, "This is My Body," does not necessarily imply any absence, or cessation, or annihilation of the substance of the outward elements. In taking them literally, we are bound to take equally in their plain

into one, as the Apollinarians and Eutychians said that the Divine and Human Natures of our Lord were consubstantial (see Vigilius c. Eut.; S. Ambr. de Incarn. c. 7, fin.; S. Ath. Ep. ad Epict. in Petav. de Inc. v. 10, 7 and 11). "Impanation" would be "a *local* inclusion of the Body of Christ in the bread." But it is taught by the Schoolmen that "our Lord's Body is *locally* in Heaven" (see in Letter to the Bishop of London, p. 73, sqq., ed. 8vo). Bellarmine (de Sacr. Euch. iii. 11), quoting Guitmundus, uses Impanation for the "hypostatic assumption of the bread by the Word," or "the mingling of the Body of Christ with the bread."

[5] See note A at the end.   [6] See note B, ib.

[7] Ed. Germ.   See Hospinian, Hist. Sacram. P. ii. p. 155, sqq.

sense His other words, in which He calls what He had just consecrated to be sacramentally His Blood, "this fruit of the vine;" or, again, those other words of Holy Scripture; "the Bread which we break;" "as often as ye eat this Bread;" "whosoever shall eat this Bread;" "so let him eat that Bread;" "we are all partakers of that one Bread." Our Blessed Lord, through those words, "This is My Body," teaches us that which it concerns us to know, His own precious Gift, the means of union and incorporation with Himself, whereby He hallows us, nourishes our souls to life everlasting, re-forms our nature and conforms it to His own; re-creates us to newness of life; binds and cements us to Himself as Man; washes, beautifies, kindles our minds, strengthens our hearts; is a source of life within us, joining us to Himself our Life, and giving us the victory over sin and death. Yet He did not deny what Himself and Holy Scripture elsewhere seem in equally plain language to affirm.

It is no unusual way of teaching in Holy Scripture, to speak of that *only*, which is at the time meant to be declared or impressed upon us. Almighty God does not, in the way of those laboured statements which we are sometimes compelled to make, guard His own words so as to express in each the whole of His truth, or preclude absolutely their being misunderstood. Thus Holy Scripture says, "Man became a living soul;" without implying that he ceased to be material. Again, when

B

Adam, under inspiration, says, "This is now bone of my bone, and flesh of my flesh," he speaks of that which Eve derived from him, and not of that which, besides, God, by His creative power, "builded" her up to be, or of the soul which He infused into her.

Again, "to those who believe, to them gave He power to become the sons of God [8]," yet did they not thereby cease to be, as men, common men. "The kingdoms of this world are become the kingdoms of our Lord, and of His Christ[9]," without thereby ceasing to be earthly kingdoms.

Or, to take a more awful instance, in order to inculcate the amazing condescension of the Incarnation, God says, "the Word became Flesh;" designating our human nature by that which is meanest in us, and most degraded. Apollinaris raised his heresy on an exclusive interpretation of the words, as though our Lord had taken flesh only, and not a human soul also. Another blasphemy, which might be raised in the same way, is guarded against in the Athanasian Creed: "not by conversion of the Godhead into flesh, but by taking the Manhood into God." "The Word became flesh," "not by conversion of substance," because He, being God, is Unchangeable; but by taking upon Him our real Human Flesh in the form of a servant.

Nor, again, are we entitled to make any one statement of Holy Scripture, exclusively, the rule for all

[8] John i. 12.   [9] Rev. xi. 15.

the rest. Such has ever been the ground of heresy. The Arians rested their dogma on our Lord's Words: " My Father is greater than I," and applied them to our Lord's Divine, not, as the orthodox, either to His Human Nature, or to His Person, as, in order, not in time, coming after the Father's [1].

Every heresy almost has been built upon some insulated statement in God's Word. God inculcates at one time, one side of Divine truth; at another, another: in order that our finite human minds may grasp, in their degree, truth after truth, and each may sink more deeply in our souls. God rarely teaches together the Divinity of our Blessed Lord, and His Humanity. The very words which contain both in one most plainly, have become the occasion of deadly heresy. We have to prove separately the Divinity of God the Holy Ghost and His Personality. Prophecy declared together our Lord's state of humiliation, and the " glory which should follow." It united also the glory which He had before the world was, and the glory which His Human Nature should have. It does not unite His previous Glory, " Mighty God, Everlasting Father," and His Atoning Death. The Jews rejected our Lord, and then invented their fable of two Messiahs, because they knew not how to blend the separate truths, and waited not patiently to see how our Lord would unite them. In their unbe-

[1] See Bull, Def. Fid. Nic. ii. 5. 8 ; iv. 2. 8, 9. Petav. de Trin. ii. 2, 2.

lief they were the instruments of blending what they thought God could not blend.

Again, misbelievers have scoffed, because the mysteries of the Unity of God and of the Holy Trinity, are thus declared in separate passages.

And so as to man, and the gifts of God to man. He speaks of the Church as "without spot or wrinkle," and of all Christians, as saints; yet elsewhere of the tares and the wheat, "the many called, and the few chosen." Our Lord says: "I will be with you always even unto the end of the world;" and asks: "When the Son of Man cometh, shall He find faith on the earth?" He speaks to us, as if our salvation were secure, and His sheep could not perish, and yet, as if all depended upon ourselves. He speaks as if for those who "sin wilfully, after that they have received the knowledge of the truth," there were nothing left but a "fearful looking for of judgment[2];" and yet He says: "Come unto Me, *all* that are weary and heavy laden, and I will give you rest." He tells us at one time, that we are "justified by faith;" at another, "by works." He tells us that "faith saveth," that we are saved by the Name of Christ, by grace, by the washing of regeneration, or by Baptism, by, or in hope, and that he who turneth "a sinner from the error of his way, shall save a soul from death[3]." And yet all these,

[2] Heb. x. 26, 27.

[3] Eph. ii. 5. Acts iv. 12. Tit. iii. 5. Rom. viii. 24. James v. 20.

and other separate fragments of teaching, unite and
blend in one whole of living truth ; as the scattered
rays of the sun in the, whole earth centre in one
glorious orb, or as the rich colours of His bow unite
in the colourless light, which gives light, and colour,
and beauty, and life unto all which lives.

We cannot, then, infer that our Blessed Lord's
words, " This is My Body," convey His whole teaching as to the Holy Eucharist. They declare one
truth ; they deny none. They affirm what It is;
they do not deny It to be also physically what It
was, any more than the great words, " the Word
became flesh," imply that the Unchangeable under-
went change ; or the saying, " Man became a living
soul," implies that he was not also flesh. Our
Blessed Lord does not say, " This is a figure of My
absent Body," nor does He say, " This has altogether ceased to be bread, and is the same Body in the
same way, as that which you see with your bodily
eyes ;" but simply: " This is My Body."

The Presence, of which our Lord speaks, has been
termed Sacramental, supernatural, mystical, ineffable,
as opposed *not* to what is real, but to what is natural. The word has been chosen to express, not our
knowledge, but our ignorance; or that unknowing
knowledge of faith, which we have of things Divine,
surpassing knowledge. We know not the manner
of His Presence, save that it is not according to the
natural Presence of our Lord's Human Flesh, which
is at the Right Hand of God ; and therefore it is

called Sacramental. But it is a Presence without us, not within us only; a Presence by virtue of our Lord's words, although to us it becomes a saving Presence, received to our salvation, through our faith. It is not a Presence simply in the soul of the receiver, as "Christ dwells in our hearts by faith;" or as, in acts of Spiritual, apart from Sacramental, Communion, we, by our longings, invite Him into our souls. But while the consecrated elements, as we believe (because our Lord and God the Holy Ghost in Holy Scripture call them still after consecration by the names of their natural substances, and do not say that they cease to be such),— while the consecrated elements remain in their natural substances, still, since our Lord says, "This is My Body," "This is My Blood," the Church of England believes that "under the form of Bread and Wine," so consecrated, we "receive the Body and Blood of our Saviour Christ [4]." And since we receive them, they must be there, in order that we may receive them. We need not then (as the School of Calvin bids men) "ascend into Heaven, to bring down Christ from above." For He is truly present, for us truly to receive Him to the salvation of our souls, if they be prepared by repentance, faith, love, through the cleansing of His Spirit, for His Coming.

Both interpretations of His sacred words, as well that which says, " This is not bread, and nothing

---

[4] Homilies, l. c.

else but His Body," and that other, "This is a figure of His absent Body," introduce that into them, which does not lie in them. Christ hath said; "This is my Body;" He saith not, by what mode. We believe what He, the Truth, saith. Truth cannot lie. How He bringeth it to pass, we may leave to His Omnipotency. It is a law which He hath impressed upon physical nature, that two bodies cannot be in the same place at the same time. And yet we receive, without doubting, that our Lord, in His spiritual Body, passed, on the morning of the Resurrection, through the sealed tomb. For the Angels rolled away the stone to show that He *was* risen[5]. He passed through the closed doors, so that the disciples thought that "it was a Spirit," as He had passed before, *illæsa virginitate,* through the doors of the Virgin's womb[6]. We do not stay to inquire in what way the substance of His Body passed through the substance of the closed doors. Enough that God has said it. As it passed, it must have been in the same place, penetrating, but not displacing them. Still less need we ask, by what law of nature, that Sacramental Presence can be, which is

[5] ἠγέρθη. See on these miracles, note C, at the end.

[6] This is stated in the Allocut. Conc. Chalc., Par. 3, T. iv. p. 1763, ed. Col.; and, of individual Fathers, by S. Irenæus, S. Clem. Alex., S. Greg. Nyss., Theodoret; and of the Latins, S. Ambrose, S. Augustine (although the homilies quoted are spurious), S. Paulinus, Gaudentius, S. Leo, Ep. 28. ad Flavian, c. 4, Maximus Taur. Hom. 2. de Nat. Christi, B. P. vi. 5. See in Petav. de Incarn. 14, 6.

not after the order of nature, but is above nature. "As [7] all things whatsoever God made, He made by the operation of the Holy Spirit, so also now, the operation of the Spirit worketh that which is above nature, which faith alone can receive. 'How shall this be to me,' said the Blessed Virgin, 'seeing that I know not a man?' Gabriel the Archangel answereth, 'The Holy Ghost shall come upon thee, and the power of the Highest shall overshadow thee.' And now askest thou, how," under these outward forms, we receive the Body of Christ, and the Blood of Christ? "The Holy Spirit cometh down and worketh what is above discourse and above all thought."

This acknowledgment of our ignorance is a refuge from our perplexity about the things of God. We acknowledge, since Scripture saith it, that the natural substance remains. "What was bread remains bread; and what was wine remains wine [8]." But faith regards

---

[7] This passage is, with one alteration, S. John Damascene's (de Fide, iv. 13, p. 269). Using the words, but not directly quoting them, I thought it best, considering the circumstances under which I preached, and the power which existed, of condemning me unheard, to substitute the formula in the Homilies for that of the original. The original does not express the doctrine of Transubstantiation (see further, App. note Q), but it might have perhaps been so understood. In the original, instead of "how, under these outward forms, we receive the Body of Christ and the Blood of Christ," it stands, "how the bread becometh the Body of Christ, and the wine and water the Blood of Christ."

[8] Newman's Sermons, vol. iv. p. 167. "We need," he added,

not things visible, only or chiefly; as it regarded not
the outward dress of our Lord, save when it touched
the hem of His garment, and virtue went out of Him,
and healed those who touched in faith[9]. Yea rather,
faith forgets things outward in His unseen Presence.
What is precious to the soul is its Redeemer's Presence, and its union with Him. It acknowledges,
yet is not anxious about, the presence of the visible
symbols. It pierces beyond the vail. It sees Him
who is invisible, and receives Him in the ruined
mansion of the soul; and by Him is strengthened;
in Him has peace; in His Presence has the pledge
of forgiveness and of everlasting union with its Lord
and its God. It owns as a truth of fact, and as
taught in God's word, the presence of the outward
symbols. Its joy, the contentment of its longings,
its hope, its strength, its stay, its peace, its life, is
the Presence of its Lord.

But as, on the one hand, it is an unauthorized
inference from our Lord's words, that the bread and
wine are no longer there; so also, and even more, is
it, that the words mean only, " This represents, is a
figure of, My absent Body." It is true that the

" no carnal, earthly, visible miracle to convince us of the Presence of the Lord Incarnate. He Who is at the Right Hand of
God, manifests Himself in that Holy Sacrament as really and
fully as if He were visibly there. We are allowed to draw near,
to 'give, take, and eat' His sacred Body and Blood, as truly as
though, like Thomas, we could touch His Hands, and thrust our
hand into His Side."

[9] S. Matt. ix. 20—22 ; xiv. 36.

outward elements are, as some of the Fathers call them, figures, types, symbols, images of His Body. But who authorized men to add, " of His absent Body?" Albeit our Lord speaks of nothing carnal or physical, who has revealed to man that when He said, " This is My Body," He meant that it was not His Body [10]?

All things combine to make us take our Lord's words solemnly and literally. All around is solemn and literal. " I hold it," says Hooker [1], " for a most infallible rule, in expositions of Holy Scripture, that when the literal construction will stand, the furthest from the literal is commonly the worst." Why should it not stand? Because it is impossible? " In mysteries," says a father, " we must believe simply; for therefore are they mysteries."

It was His last parting act, the anticipation of His Passion, His Testament in His Blood, His gift to His own in the stead of His own Visible Presence, a new revelation, applying and embodying in act what He had before taught, "Except ye eat the Flesh of the Son of Man, and drink His Blood, ye have no life in you." "Whoso eateth My Flesh, and drinketh My Blood, hath everlasting life."

The solemnity of the words is enforced by the

---

[10] S. Cyril of Jerus., Lect. 22, § 2, p. 270, Oxf. Tr. " Since then He Himself has declared and said of the Bread, ' *This is My Body*,' who shall dare to doubt any longer? And since He has affirmed and said, ' *This is My Blood*,' who shall ever hesitate, saying, that it is not His Blood? "　　　 [1] E. P. v. 59, 2.

almost unvarying uniformity with which they are recorded. God has appointed that four inspired writers should deliver to us the words of Institution. They repeat with an awful oneness, His action, His blessing, His gift, His words. S. Matthew, S. Mark, S. Luke, and S. Paul, to whom our Lord revealed it from Heaven, say alike; " He took bread, He blessed, He brake, He gave it. He said, Take, eat, this is My Body." " He took the cup, He blessed, He gave it to them, He said, This is My Blood of the New Testament." The very words, " This is My Blood of the New Testament," are framed upon those whereby the old Covenant at Mount Sinai was sanctioned through the sprinkling of real blood of a sacrifice, appointed by God to shadow out the Atoning Blood which was shed upon the Cross. " And Moses took the blood, and sprinkled it on the people, and said, Behold the blood of the covenant, which the Lord hath made with you concerning all these words [2]." S. Paul contrasts the figures with the substance, " the blood of others," with which the first testament was dedicated, and " the Blood of Christ, who through the eternal Spirit offered Himself without spot to God." The blood of the Old Testament was a shadow, not in itself, but in its value. It was the real, although unavailing, blood of bulls and goats, picturing that the Atonement should be through the shedding of the Precious Blood of Christ. But the picture itself

[2] Exod. xxiv. 8.

was real blood. When then our Blessed Lord, recalling the sanction of the Old Testament, by the very form of the words, added to them, "This is *My* Blood of the New Testament, which is shed for you and for many, for the remission of sins;" what else could the Apostles think, but that our Lord meant, that it was really and truly, and, in a Divine way, His Blood, and that they now and henceforth should in a new and nearer way be united with Him and live by Him, as He Himself had promised, " He that eateth My Flesh, and drinketh My Blood, dwelleth in Me and I in him?" " Was it possible they should hear that Voice, ' Take, eat, this is My Body; drink ye all of this, this is My Blood;' possible that doing what was required and believing what was promised, the same should have present effect in them, and not fill them with a kind of fearful admiration at the heaven which they saw in themselves [3]?"

When our Lord, for the hardness of men's hearts, spake in parables, He Himself expounded all things [4] privately to His disciples. The Evangelists themselves at times, explain when He spake in a figure [5]; or the very language itself marks itself to be a parable. Our Lord in that solemn hour was completing the shadows of the law. Why should we think that He brought in a mere shadow, less expressive than those which He abolished? He, our good Master,

[3] Hooker, E. P. v. 67, § 4.   [4] Mark iv. 34.
[5] John ii. 19. 21 ; vii. 38, 39 ; vi. 70, 71.

was leaving " His Testament " in His Blood to His Disciples, even to the end of the world. We do not think that even a man, in a testament, means to leave the mere figures of what he professes to bestow. Human principles of interpretation require that we should believe that a testator means what he says [6]. Reverence for the word of God requires, that we should not tamper with its apparent meaning, on any preconceived notions of our own.

In those words which men are wont to quote, Holy Scripture itself informs us that there *is* a figure, so often as there is one, lest we should exchange the substance for figures. Holy Scripture, in speaking of Almighty God, is full of figures. Well-nigh every thing which is said of Him, unless it be a simple declaration of His Attributes, as that He is Just, Holy, Good, must be a figure, expressing some reality. The very qualities of Almighty God are expressed to us in figures, borrowed from those qualities in man, which are some shadow of them. For patience, long-suffering, compassion, and the like, much more anger or jealousy, imply literally some passion, which cannot be in God [7]. To speak of

[6] See note D, at the end.

[7] This is still more expressed in the sacred language, in which God condescends not only to attribute to Himself the quality, but to speak of it under metaphors describing its effects on man. " The anger of the Lord smoked " (Deut. xxix. 20); " was kindled," frequently ; " went up," Ps. lxxviii. 21 (compare 2 Sam. xi. 20, of man), " slow of wrath ;" " my soul loathed them " (literally, " was shortened for them," Zech. xi. 8); as

" attributes " at all, is to speak in figure ; for God is One, Simple, Undivided Essence, in Whom Love is not separate from Justice, nor Holiness from Mercy, as in us the qualities of our mind balance and correct one another. In Him all is one. It is a just, holy, wise, good Love. Love of good and hatred of evil are one and the same in Him. To us they are different aspects of His All-Holy Love.

Abstract terms go but a little way in declaring to us the ways of God. He mirrors Himself in the works of His Hands. He stamps in the book of His Word the meaning of the book of His works. Even the works of men's hands, as being formed by minds which are made in the Image of God, in some way reflect His Image. The orders and ranks of earthly polity, as far as they proceed on the rules of eternal right, proceed from Him and reflect Him. The ritual of the Old Testament was prescribed, the history of the chosen people was overruled, to foreshadow that which was to come. All is one great picture-language, to make present to our senses and minds what is invisible, intangible, inconceivable.

Whether then our Lord be called a Lion, a Lamb, a Rock, a Hiding-place, a Fountain, a Vine,

expressing in man unendurance, impatience. On the other hand, the tenderest word expressing the mercy of God, describes Him as yearning over us. The very word, from which the σπλάγχνα ἐλέους of the New Testament is taken, is even chiefly used of God. But this is a further use of metaphor. The plainest words are still figures, if, as they mostly are, they are taken from any quality in man.

a Door, a Branch, a King, a Judge, a Priest, a Shepherd, these are but different letters of the one great alphabet of that condescending language in which God reveals Himself to man. It is, then, altogether a mistake to lay stress on any such condescending words of our Lord as "I am the Door;" "I am the true Vine." They are instances of the great picture-language of Holy Scripture, of just the same sort as when our Lord adds, "My Father is the Husbandman;" "I am the good Shepherd;" or, again, "I am Alpha and Omega;" "I am the bright and morning Star." "Am" does not in these cases signify "being the figure of," but the converse. The Door and the Vine are figures of our Lord. "Is" in Holy Scripture is used alike in figurative or in plain language; "I am the Door," as well as "the Word was God." It is used to join the two thoughts together, by which, whether in plain or figurative words, God wills to declare some truth. The figurative meaning does not lie in the word "is," but in the picture-word joined with it. Nor is there any case in Holy Scripture in which, being figurative, it is not indicated in the context that it *is* figurative [8]. The words "I am the true vine," "I am the door of the sheep," occur in parables. S. Paul does not say, "that Rock was Christ," until he had before said, "that spiritual rock [9];" showing that he spake in a figure. When he says, "Agar is Mount Sinai in Arabia," he says also, "it is an allegory."

[8] See note E, at the end.   [9] 1 Cor. x. 4.

But the word "Body" is no figure. For our Lord says, "This is *My* Body;" and not so only, but "this is My Body which is given for you." Since, then, it was His true Body which was given *for* us upon the Cross, it is His true Body which is given *to* us in the Sacrament [1]. The manner of the Presence of the Body is different. The Body which is present is the same, for He has said, "This is My Body which is given for you."

S. Paul's words are an expansion and application of our Lord's. Our Lord says, "This is My Body;" S. Paul, "Is it not the Communion of the Body of Christ?" Our Lord says, "This is My Blood;" S. Paul, "Is it not the Communion of the Blood of Christ?" There is no bond between a communion and a figure. Had the Holy Eucharist been only a figure, there would be nothing whereof It could be a communion. True, what we see, in that it is broken, is an image of His Body which was slain;

---

[1] Of the Calvinistic theory even Beza says, "Certainly it would be too absurd to interpret the names of the Body and Blood of the fruit and efficacy of the Death of the Lord, or to restrain them to the spiritual object thereof alone. To make this perfectly plain, let us substitute that interpretation for these words, 'Body' and 'Blood,' and say, 'This is the efficacy of My death, which is given for you, and this is My Spirit which is poured out for you.' What more senseless than such a mode of speaking? For certainly those words, 'which is given for you,' of necessity constrain men to understand it of the very substance of the Body and Blood of Christ."—Epist. 5. ad Aleman, p. 57, ed. Gen., quoted by Gerhard, loci 22, c. 10.

and in that it is poured out, is an image of His Blood which was shed. That which is seen is an image of the reality which is unseen. Yet God says not by S. Paul it is an image, but it is " the communion of the Body of Christ." But, in order to be a communion of It,. there must be That of which it is the communion. " Why," asks S. Chrysostom², ": did he not say ' participation ?' (μετοχή.) Because He wished to point out something more, to show how great is the conjunction (συνάφεια). For we communicate, not by sharing only and partaking, but also by being united. For as that Body is united to Christ, so also are we united to Him by this Bread." S. Chrysostom, no more than the Church of England, had any thought of what is physical or carnal. When we too are taught to pray that we " may so eat the Flesh of Christ, and drink His Blood, that our sinful bodies may be made clean by His Body, and our souls washed through His most Precious Blood," we mean a real, actual, though Sacramental and spiritual drinking ; we do not mean a figurative cleansing by a figurative eating and drinking.

But in that we press the literal meaning of these words of our Lord and of S. Paul, we do, in fact, bind ourselves to take with equal strictness those other words of both : " this fruit of the vine," and " this bread." If one might be taken figuratively, so might the other. If, as the Genevan school would have it, the words " this is my Body " were figura-

² Ad loc. Hom. 24, § 4, p. 327, Oxf. Tr.

tive, or if, as Roman Divines say, S. Paul's words were figurative, " the bread which we break," it would be but consistent to say with some modern sectaries, that the words " so let him eat of that bread, and drink of that cup," are figurative too.

Our Lord does not say more distinctly, " This is My Blood of the New Testament which is shed for many for the remission of sins," than He subjoins immediately, " I will not drink henceforth of this fruit of the vine, until that day when I drink it new with you in my Father's Kingdom." He says as plainly, " this fruit of the vine[3]," as He had said, " This is My Blood." He says both. We believe both.

Again, whatever else our Lord may have meant by " drinking this fruit of the vine new in the king-dom of My Father," the literal sense can scarcely be excluded. The literal does not exclude the spiritual, but is the basis of it. The Apostles, in proof of the reality of the Resurrection, lay stress on the fact, that they " *did* eat and drink with Him after He rose from the dead." Most probably, our Lord was preparing the souls of His disciples to look for Him again after His Death, which they could not bear to think of or believe, and spake of being again with them as before, only in a new way. If, by the kingdom of God He means, at least in its beginnings, that kingdom which He set up after His Resurrection, when He says, " All power is given to

[3] See on this text, note F, at the end.

Me in Heaven and in earth;" and by the drinking of the fruit of the vine or wine then, He means in part, the taking natural food with them, in proof of His Resurrection; then it would be unnatural to understand Him as not speaking of what was a natural substance then. We could not paraphrase His words, " I will not drink this, which was wine once, but is so no longer, until, after My Resurrection, I drink it new in its natural substance." Roman controversialists alternately concede, that " the fruit of the vine" does mean the natural substance of wine ; only then they maintain it not to have been said of the wine just consecrated, but of common wine ; or they concede it to be (as S. Matthew distinctly shows that it is) used of that of which He had just said, " This is My Blood," and say that it means the accidents of wine only. Each grants *that* part of the natural meaning which he can afford. The one, that " the fruit of the vine" is to be understood of the natural substance; the other, that the words which our Lord uttered immediately after the consecration of the Cup, refer to that "fruit of the vine" which He had just consecrated. Put the two together, and you cannot escape the inference : *therefore*, that which He had just consecrated was still, physically and in its natural substance, the natural fruit of the vine.

There is then no ground from Holy Scripture to make the language of our Lord or S. Paul figurative, whether as to the outward elements, that we should

think that the bread and wine cease to be in their
natural substances, or as to the real inward spiritual
Presence of His Body and Blood, whereby our
good Lord in His unutterable love "dwells in us,
and we in Him, is one with us, and we with Him."
The Catholic Fathers, to whom our Canon[4] refers
as our guides in understanding Holy Scripture, take
both alike literally. "It is not to be denied," says
Thorndike [5], "that all Ecclesiastical writers do, with
one mouth, bear witness to the Presence of the
Body and Blood of Christ in the Eucharist. Neither will any one of them be found to ascribe it to
any thing but the Consecration; or *that*, to any faith
but that upon which the Church professeth to proceed to the celebrating of it. And upon this account, when they speak of the elements, supposing
the Consecration to have passed upon them, they
always call them by the name, not of their bodily
substance, but of the Body and Blood of Christ
which they are become." "But this change," he
says [6], "is not destructive to the bodily substance of
the elements, but cumulative of them with the
spiritual grace of Christ's Body and Blood."

It should be added, that when the Fathers speak
of the elements as remaining, they are most often
speaking very accurately, in the illustration of the

[4] Canon about Preachers enacted in Convocation, A.D. 1571.

[5] Epilogue, B. 3, c. 4, pp. 30—33, § 27, p. 69, ed. Angl.
Cath. Lib.

[6] Ib. § 45, p. 82.

faith against heresy. When they are speaking de-
votionally of the wonderfulness of God's Gift, it is
natural that they should speak only of that gift
itself, the Presence of Christ, and the actual impart-
ing of His Body and Blood, not of the outward
elements, through which that gift is conveyed.

Thus, on the one side, S. Irenæus, against heretics
who denied the Resurrection of the body[7], says:
"Bread from the earth, receiving the invocation of
God, is no longer common bread, but the Eucharist,
consisting of two things, an earthly and a heavenly."
Tertullian[8], against the Gnostics, says: "The bread
taken and distributed to the disciples, He made
that His own Body, saying: 'This is My Body,' i. e.
the figure of My Body. But it would not be a
figure, unless His Body were a true Body." Tertullian believed the elements to be a figure too of
His Body, not as absent, but as present. He argues
from the reality of the figure to the reality of the
thing figured. There could be no real figure of that
which had no real substance. But unless the natural substance really remained, the figure itself, i. e.
the accidents, would also be a phantom. Had the
Church then believed that the elements were accidents without substance, the Gnostics might have
retorted: " unsubstantial accidents are an appro-
priate figure of such a Body as we conceive, un-

[7] The following passages from the Fathers on this head are
given more fully, and any questions which have been raised as to
some, are considered in note G, at the end.

[8] Adv. Marcion, iv. 20.

substantial." Again, against the same heretics who rejected matter, he speaks of the physical substance of bread, as the outward visible means of the one Sacrament, just as he does of the physical substance of water in the other great Sacrament; or of the oil, honey, milk, in other rites of the Church. Again, in that he says, " He makes His Body present *by* the bread," he asserts the presence of that bread, whereby He makes It present. Another[9] argues against the same heretics: " If, as these say, He was fleshless and bloodless, of what flesh, or of what body, and of what blood, did He, giving the *images*, enjoin upon the disciples both the bread and the cup?" S. Chrysostom argues against the Apollinarians from the twofold substance in the Holy Eucharist, and says that after Consecration, "the nature of bread remains in it." Theodoret, against the Eutychians, says: " Neither after Consecration do the mystic symbols depart from their own nature; they remain in their former substance; He doth not change the nature, but adds grace to the nature." Pope Gelasius says that " the elements abide in their own proper nature." Facundus, against the Adoptians: " The Sacrament of His Body and Blood which is in the consecrated Bread and Cup, we call His Body and Blood; not that the Bread is properly His Body, or the Cup His Blood, but because they contain in them the mystery of His Body and Blood." Ephrem of Antioch against the Euty-

---

[9] Adamantius, probably about the age of Constantine. See Benedictine Præf. T. i. p. 800-2. ed. De la Rue.

chians: "The Body of Christ which is received by the faithful, neither departeth from the sensible substance, nor is separable from the invisible grace."

Again, when great writers, as S. Athanasius, S. Justin Martyr, S. Irenæus, or S. Cyril [10], say that they are not "*bare* elements," not "*common* bread," nor "*mere* bread and a *mere* cup," it is plain that they must have believed them, as we do, to be still real elements in their natural substances; and that the more, since they use the same words of the water of Baptism or the oil of the Chrism.

Again, when others, as S. Basil, S. Gregory of Nazianzum, S. Macarius, Eusebius, Theodoret, Eustathius, S. Augustine[1], say, as did Tertullian, that the consecrated elements are symbols, types, antitypes, figures, images of our Lord's Body and Blood, as it is clear from their own writings that they did *not* mean figures of an *absent* body, so also is it that they did mean, that there was a real visible substance which was the image or symbol of the *present* spiritual, invisible substance.

Again, the emblem of the burning coal with which Isaiah's lips were hallowed, which was received throughout the East (in S. Ephrem and S. James of Sarug, in S. Chrysostom and Theodoret, in the Liturgies of S. James, S. Chrysostom, and S. Cyril [2]),

---

[10] See the passages in Note H.

[1] See the passages in Note I.

[2] See the passages in Note K.

implies an inward real Presence, and a real outward substance. Whence S. Ephrem often speaks of our Lord's Presence, under the image of "fire *in* the bread [3]." "*In* Thy visible vesture there dwelleth a hidden power." "*In* Thy Bread is hidden.the Spirit that cannot be eaten. *In* Thy Wine there dwelleth the Fire that cannot be drunk. Instead of that fire which devoured men, ye eat the fire *in* Bread and are quickened." "*In* the Bread and the Cup are fire and the Holy Ghost." "We have eaten Thee, we have drunken Thee, not that we shall make Thee fail, but that we might have life in Thee. Thy garment covered Thy feebler nature: the bread covereth the fire which dwells therein [4]."

Tertullian [5] says, "*In* the bread is understood His Body." S. Augustine [6] says, "Our Lord Jesus Christ commended His Body and Blood *in* those things which are, out of many [many grains and many grapes], reduced into some one." S. James of Sarug [7], "He from whom the spirits of fire have their glow, Him *in* Bread and Wine thou seest on the Table."

Again, so literally did early Fathers take the words "this fruit of the vine," that it was the foundation of the doctrine of the Millennium, so

[3] P. 146, Oxf. Tr.
[4] See the passages in Note L.
[5] De Orat. c. 6, p. 303, Oxf. Tr.
[6] In Joann. Tract. 26, No. 17.
[7] In Ass. Bibl. Or. T. iii. p. 326.

largely held in the early centuries, while not a few make some inference from it, to establish the use of wine in the Holy Eucharist, or as a proof of the Resurrection [8].

Again, it was a philosophy well known to the Fathers, that accidents do not nourish, and that they do not exist separate from their substance; and yet they simply assume that the elements are converted into the substance of the human body, and do nourish it. S. Justin Martyr, a philosopher before he was converted, says, in one and the same place, that the bread and wine of the Holy Eucharist are not *common* bread and wine, (and so, surely that they are bread and wine,) and that they are the Body and Blood of our Incarnate Lord; and that from this food our flesh and blood are by change [into our substance] nourished [9].

Again, the Fathers use undoubtingly the word which we have in our services, "spiritually," opposed as it is, not to really and sacramentally, but to physically and carnally. Thus S. Clement of Alexandria [1]: " Wherefore the Saviour, having first taken bread, spake and gave thanks. Then, having broken the bread, He placed it before them, that we may eat reasonably." S. Athanasius [2]: " On this ground He

[8] See further in Note M.

[9] Apol. i. 66, p. 83. Tertullian also says, " The flesh feedeth on the Body and Blood of Christ, that the soul too may be nourished from God."—*De Res. Carn.* § 8.

[1] Strom. 1, 10, p. 343, ed. Pott.   [2] Ep. iv. ad Serap. § 19, p. 710.

mentioned the Ascent of the Son of Man into Heaven, that He might withdraw them from corporeal thoughts, and that they might understand that the Flesh spoken of was spiritual Food from above, and spiritual nourishment given by Him." S. Macarius [3]: "They who partake of the visible bread, spiritually eat the Flesh of the Lord." S. Ambrose [4]: "In that sacrament Christ is, because it is Christ's Body; it is not, therefore, bodily food, but spiritual. Whence also the Apostle says of its type: 'our fathers ate a spiritual food, and drank a spiritual drink;' for the Body of God is a spiritual Body: the Body of Christ is Body of a Divine Spirit; for Christ is a Spirit." S. Augustine: "Eat Life, drink Life; thou shalt have life, and the life is entire. But then shall the Body and the Blood of Christ be each man's life, if what is taken in the Sacrament visibly is, in the truth itself, eaten spiritually, drunk spiritually [5]."

To add some single expressions [6]: a near disciple of S. Ambrose says, that the elements "both are what they were, and are changed into something else." Physically they are what they were: sacramentally they are the Body and Blood of Christ. Origen speaks of the matter of bread "remaining in the food consecrated by the Word of God." S. Au-

---

[3] Hom. 27, § 17, p. 164.
[4] De Myst. fin. § 58.
[5] See the passages in Note P.
[6] See the passages at length in Note O.

gustine says, " One thing is seen, another understood. What is seen, hath a bodily form; what is understood, hath a spiritual fruit." S. Epiphanius speaks of superadded power, " *That which is seen is round and insensate as to power*. He willed to say by grace ' This is of Me that, and no one disbelieveth His Word.' The Bread is food, but the power in it is to the giving of life [7]." S. Hilary: " We received the Word, made Flesh, through the food of the Lord." The food *through* which we receive It is surely real.

Nor does it in any way weaken the force of this proof, that several of the Fathers use such words as transmute, trans-make, transform, trans-element, re-order, of the working of the consecration, nor again that they illustrate that working by other Divine operations, some of which are physical changes.

Those words do not express the doctrine of the scholastic Divines. They do not express change of substance (for μεταστοιχείωσις is not used in its etymological meaning), while the word now used of change of substance was then unknown. And further, all these words are also, by the very same Fathers, used of spiritual changes, which do not involve change of substance, and in some of which to suppose a change of substance would be blasphemy, or would contradict an article of faith.

In the same context, in which a Father speaks of

---

[7] Ancor. c. 57, Expos. Fid. Cath. c. 16, p. 1096.

the sacramental change, he says, using the same word, " The Body [of Christ] by the indwelling of God the Word, was trans-made, μετεποιήθη, into the Divine dignity."

More largely, the Fathers speak of the change and " transmuting of the human nature into the Divine;" they say that " the Lord's Body was *trans-elemented* into incorruption;" "the Flesh of our Lord *becometh* Christ and Lord;" " the Flesh of the Manhood was *trans-made* into the Divine Nature;" " what was visible *became* Christ and Lord."

More frequently yet do they use the words of a change which is wholly spiritual, the change of regeneration. " Our nature is by Baptism," they say, " transformed from corruptible to incorruptible;" " spiritually trans-elemented from a foul to a better state;" " trans-elemented to the ancient image through the Spirit;" "trans-elemented to that which was above nature." Again they say; " repentance trans-makes nature;" " habits are new-made into nature;" " instruction re-orders the man;" the body is raised again the very same, but is trans-made, trans-elemented into incorruption. They use the illustration [8]; " iron (red hot) *becometh* fire." They say: " we are *changed* into the substance of angels;" " the body *passeth* into the nature of the soul;" " nature is *changed* into a heavenly substance;" " saints are *changed* into angels;" " Chris-

---

[8] See further, Note Q.

tians are wholly *trans-elemented* into Christ, Who hath power to impart life."

Again, the object of the likenesses used by the Fathers, is either to illustrate the power of God, as put forth in our behalf, in things which we know, that we may not start back at the greatness of His gift in the Holy Eucharist, or to show how things, outwardly the same, may be inwardly, yet spiritually, not physically, changed, or how grace may be conveyed through visible symbols[9]. But it does not therefore follow that they held the change to be of the same nature, or in the same degree. If the likeness were unduly pressed on the one side, as in the Miracle of Cana, it would be inferred that one physical substance was changed into another, not previously existing; which would be heretical. If other likenesses were pressed, it might be inferred that there was only an outward consecration, without any spiritual change or any inward sacred Presence. S. Gregory of Nyssa, cited in proof of transubstantiation, illustrates the grace of Baptism, by the holiness of an Altar, the change in the Holy Eucharist, the oil of confirmation, the consecration of a priest, the rod of Moses, the mantle of Elijah, the wood of the Cross, the bush where God was seen. These are valid to the end for which S. Gregory quotes them, that God uses the mean things of this world in showing forth His own glory. But

---

[9] See further, Note R.

since the changes are of every sort, nothing can be inferred as to the nature of that change. The Altar has but an outward sanctity. The bush was but the place of a miracle. Elijah's mantle once, Moses' rod oftentimes, were the instruments of God's miraculous power. The Wood of the Cross was the instrument, not of a miracle, but of the all-Atoning Sacrifice. The Priest is not, of necessity, inwardly sanctified. The rod, when changed into a serpent, was changed in outward form also. So far was S. Gregory from contemplating a physical change, that he, as well as others, compares together the sacred oil, and the wine of the Holy Eucharist. No one of these likenesses fully agrees with the Holy Eucharist. In pressing one point, people have forgotten that.others might be pressed in the opposite way. They overlook the rule which holds in interpreting our Lord's own Divine parables, where He Himself frames and points out the likeness, viz. that the likeness is not to be extended beyond the direct scope and intention of the parable itself.

On both grounds it may be assumed, that the Fathers did not intend to assert any physical change in the material substance; and when they asserted, as they do continually, that what is consecrated and what we receive, are the Body and Blood of Christ, they mean this, not in any physical or carnal way, but spiritually, sacramentally, Divinely, mystically, ineffably, through the operation of the Word of Christ, and of God the Holy Ghost.

But, in this meaning, they do speak of the objective presence of the Body and Blood of Christ, as following upon the consecration. This they teach unvaryingly from the times of the Apostles, as strongly and as distinctly as any other portion of the Faith.

I will quote the language not of one, two, or three, not from one age or one school, but the uniform teaching of the Fathers of every Church and of every variety of mind, in every sort of writing, Epistles, Homilies, Treatises, &c., including above seventy writers of those times to which our Church teaches us to look with most reverence, and every individual whose name she has held out for our love [1].

---

[1] The authorities here quoted, together with other passages from those Fathers of whom there are larger remains, will, with God's help, be given fully in their context in the Appendix, Note 7. In the following chronological arrangement, Cave has mostly been followed:—

	A.D.		A.D.
1. S. Ignatius	101	12. S. Dionysius Alex.	247
2. S. Justin Martyr.	140	13. S. Cyprian (with Afr.	
3. S. Irenæus.	167	Council)	248
4. S. Melito	170	14. S. Laurence	257
5. Tatian	172	15. Magnes	265
6. S. Clem. Alex. } 193		16. S. Peter Alex.	301
7. Tertullian }		17. Eusebius	315
8. Inscript. Augustod.,		18. Council of Nice } 325	
end of Cent. 2.		19. S. James, Nisibis . }	
9. S. Hippolytus	220	20. Athanasius	326
10. Origen	230	21. Anonym. de Solemnit.	
11. S. Firmilian	233	22. Juvencus	330

From S. Ignatius, who speaks of "misbelievers who confess not that the Eucharist is Flesh of our

	A.D.
23. Theodor. Heracl. ...	334
24. S. Julius	337
25. Council of Alexandria	339
26. Julius Firmicus	340
27. S. Theodore, successor to S. Pachomius	344
28. Thecla and Martyrs under Sapor......	346
29. S. Cyril, Jerus. ..	
30. S. Gregory Illum. Armen.	350
31. Liberius	352
32. S. Hilary........	
33. Hilarius Diac. ...	354
34. S. Victorinus.....	
35. Titus Bostrensis ..	362
36. S. Epiphanius....	
37. S. Optatus	368
38. S. Pacian	
39. S. Ephrem, Syr.	
40. S. Basil	
41. S. Greg. Nyss. ..	
42. S. Greg. Naz. ...	370
43. Cæsarius (brother of S. Greg. Naz.)	
44. S. Amphilochius ..	
45. Apollinarius	
46. S. Didymus......	
47. Esaias Abbas	371
48. S. Macarius......	
49. Euseb. Alexandr.	373

	A.D.
50. S. Ambrose........	374
51. Auct. de Sacram. ap. S. Ambr.	
52. S. Jerome	378
53. S. Siricius	
54. S. Theophil. Al.	385
55. Jerome of Jerusalem	386
56. S. Gaudentius......	387
57. S. Isaac Mag., about	390
58. S. Paulinus, Nol.	
59. S. Maruthas (friend of S. Chrys.) ..	393
60. S. Augustine	395
61. S. Chrysostome	398
62. Council of Carthage (Stat. Eccl. Ant.)	
63. Philo Carpas. ...	401
64. Victor, Antioch.	
65. S. Chromatius......	402
66. S. Cyril, Alex. ..	
67. S. Isidore, Pelus.	412
68. Paulinus, Diac.	420
69. S. Maximus Taur. .	422
70. Theodoret	423
71. Theodot. Ancyr. ..	430
72. S. Pet. Chrysol.	433
73. S. Proclus	
74. Sedulius	434
75. S. Leo..........	
76. Salvian	440
77. S. Nilus	

Saviour Jesus Christ, the Flesh which suffered for our sins, which the Father in His mercy raised again [1];" and who says of himself, " I have no taste for corruptible food, nor for the pleasures of this life. Bread of God I desire, Heavenly Bread, Bread of Life which is Flesh of Jesus Christ; and Drink of God I desire; His Blood which is love without corruption, and life for evermore [2];"—from S. Ignatius,—the successor of an Apostle, consecrated to the see of Antioch by the hands of S. Peter,—down to S. Leo, they speak with one voice. I will rehearse to you simply their own unaltered [3] words, without mingling one of my own. They say, then, " The [4] Lord provideth for us food from Himself. He offereth Flesh, and poureth out Blood, and nothing is wanting to the children's growth." " Being [5] both Flesh and Bread, He giveth Himself, being both, to us to eat." " He is the Bread of us who appertain to His Body [6]." " His Flesh is true Food [7]."

[1] Ep. ad Smyrn. n. 7, 8.   [2] Ep. ad Rom. § 7.

[3] The grammatical form has been, in some places, altered, in order to avoid rapid changes of persons or the like.

[4] S. Clem. Al. Pædag. 1. 6, p. 123.

[5] Id. Fragm. T. ii. p. 1018, ed. Pott.

[6] S. Cyprian [13], de Orat. Dom. n. 13, p. 187, Oxf. Tr. Others render " who touch His Body ;" but I have retained the rendering as revised by Mr. Newman, since the context relates to His Mystical Body, with which we are united by Communion, and from which, by being forbidden Communion, we should be separated.

[7] Orig. [10] in Num. Hom. 7, n. 2.

"The Lord is true Bread, and His Flesh is mystical Food [1]." "He gave to believers His own Body and Blood, infusing into them the life-giving Medicine of Divinity [2]." "He gave them for food, the Heavenly Bread, Himself, [gave] Himself [3]." "To nourish us, He spares not His own Flesh and Blood [4]." ,'He giveth Himself to thee, to receive within thee [5]." "God invites us to His own table, and sets before us His own Son [6]." "Our Lord gave His own Body that they might eat, and His Blood that they might drink [7]." "He left us His own Flesh [8]." "He pours out as wine His own proper Blood [9]." "Taking the bread and then the Cup of wine, He attested that it is His Body and Blood [10]." "He embodieth Himself into food and drink, that He may ineffably rest the soul, and fill it with spiritual joy [11]." "He had consecrated the Blood of His own Body, to be poured

[1] Theodor. Heracl. [23] in Ps. 33, 9 (Corder. Cat. i. 596).

[2] Magnes [15], Fragm. § 3. Gall. iii. 541.

[3] αὐτὸς ἑαυτόν. Euseb. [17] in Ps. 80, 17, in Montfauc. Nov. Coll. i. 504. Comp. in Is. 65, 12. Ib. ii. 586.

[4] S. Chrys. [61] in ill. Vid. elig., § 15 ; T. iii. 327.

[5] Id. in S. Matt. Hom. 82, § 4, p. 1091, Oxf. Tr.

[6] Id. Hom. ii. in Nativ., § 7, T. ii. 430.

[7] S. James Nisib. [19], Serm. 14, de Pasch., n. 4, p. 342, ed. Rom.

[8] S. Chrys. Hom. 2, ad Pop. Ant., § 9, fin. [on the Statues, p. 52, 3, Oxf. Tr.]

[9] S. Amphiloch. [44], Serm. adv. Arian. in Conc. Const. Act. Maii Nov. Coll. iv. p. 10.

[10] Tatian [5], Harmon. iv. Evang. Bibl. Patr. ii., P. 2, p. 210.

[11] S. Macar. [48], Hom. iv., p. 22, ed. Par.

forth for the remission of sins[1]." "He taught the disciples that He delivered His own Body,—that He had divided [among them] His own Blood[2]." "By the declaration of the Lord Himself, and by our faith, It is truly Flesh and truly Blood; and these, received and drunk, effect that both we are in Christ and Christ is in us[3]." "From bread (because He can and hath ·promised) He maketh His own Body; of wine, His own Blood[4]." "He consecrated the two gifts of life, of His Body and Blood[5];" "gave [His servants] as Food the sinless Flesh[6]." "Christ Himself 'prepared' for the Church 'the Body' of the Lord, at the time of the Mystical Feast, when He said, Take, eat[7]." "He mingled the nature of His Flesh with the nature of Eternity, under the Sacrament of the Flesh to be communicated to us[8]." "In all who believe the economy of grace, He inserts Himself through the Flesh[9]" . . . "mingling Himself in the bodies of believers, that by the union with the Immortal, man too might become partaker

---

[1] S. Hil. [32] in S. Matt., c. 31, n. 7, p. 743.

[2] Juvencus [22], Hist. Ev. L. iv. Bibl. Patr. iv. 74.

[3] S. Hil. de Trin. viii. 14.

[4] S. Gaudent. [56] de Pasch., Tr. ii., B. P. v., p. 946.

[5] Sedulius [74], Carm. Pasch. v. 3. Gall. ix. 592.

[6] Proclus [73], Orat. x. init. Gall. ix. 655.

[7] Didymus Al. [46], ap. Corderii Cat. in Ps. 39. 7. T. i., p. 748.

[8] S. Hil. de Trin. viii. § 13.

[9] S. Greg. Nyss. [41], Orat. Catechet. (the text is that of Maii Nov. Coll. vi. 370-2.)

of incorruption." "We know that the wine is consecrated into the Blood of Christ[1]." "That which
is in the Cup is that which flowed from His side,
and thereof do we partake[2]." "He was carried in
His own Hands, when, commending His own very
Body to us, He said, 'This is My Body'[3]." "He
refreshed His Apostles with the food of His own
Body[4]." "He is really present, because the Sacrament is His Body[5]." "The Eucharist becomes
Christ's Body and Blood[6]." "The Bread becomes
the Body, and the Cup, the Blood of the Lord Jesus
Christ[7]." "That same Christ who was crucified for
us, makes them to become His Body and Blood[8]."
"The Word descends into that Bread, and that Cup,
and it becomes His Body[9]." "The Bread, consecrated with thanksgiving by the prayer of the Word
which is from Him, is (so we are taught) the Body
and Blood of that Incarnate Jesus[10]." "It is the
Divine Body which is consecrated on the Holy Table,

[1] S. Jerom. [52], L. iii. in Gal. v. 20.

[2] S. Chrys. in 1 Cor. x. 16. Hom. 24, § 3.

[3] S. Aug. [60] in Ps. 32, S. 1, § 10, p. 214.

[4] Anonym. de Solemnitat. &c., c. 6 [21], cap. Spicil. Solesm.,
p. 11, ed. Pitra.

[5] S. Chrys. in ill. Vidi Dom., § 4, vi. 165.

[6] S. Iren. [3], v. 2, 3.

[7] S. Athan. [20], Serm. ad Neoph. ap. Eutychium in Luc.
[Maii Coll. Nov. ix. 625.] See also S. Aug. Serm. 227, ad
Inf. S. Cyril Jer. [29], Cat. Myst. i. § 7.

[8] S. Chrys. de Prodit. Jud. i. 6.   [9] S. Athan., l. c.

[10] S. Justin. [2], Apol. i. 66, p. 83, ed. Ben.

and indivisibly distributed to the whole sacred band, and partaken of without ceasing to be [1]."

"We have heard the true Master, the Divine Redeemer, the tender Saviour, commending to us our Price, His Blood. He spake to us of His Body and Blood. He called His Body food; His Blood, drink [2]." "The bread becometh the Body, and the Cup becometh the Blood of the Lord [3]." "The Spirit setteth forth (ἀποφαῖνον) on the Mystic table, the common bread to be the proper Body of His Incarnation [4]." "He was laid in the Manger that He might be eaten on the Table and become to believers a saving Food [5]." "He has sanctified for ever as food for us His own Flesh [6]." "He made His Body Food for the whole world, and satisfied all the ends of the world with His life-giving Body [7]."

---

[1] S. Cæsarius (brother of S. Greg. Naz.) [43]. Dial. 3, Interrog. 169, ap. Gall. vi. 127.

[2] S. Aug. Serm. 131, in Joh. 6, T. v. p. 640 [Hom. on N. T. p. 585, Oxf. Tr.].

[3] Euseb. Alex. [49], Serm. v. in Maii Spicil. Rom. ix. p. 660.

[4] S. Isidore Pel. [67], Ep. i. 109, ad Marathon., p. 34.

[5] Theod. Anc. [71] Hom. in Nat. in Conc. Eph. P. 3, c. 9; iii. 1526, ed. Col.

[6] S. Paulin. [58] Ep. 23, ad Sever. § 7, T. i. p. 125, ed. Paris. Comp. S. Ambrose [50] de Bened. Patriarch. c. 9, n. 38. "He daily giveth us that Bread, which Himself, the Priest, daily consecrates with His own words." Auct. de Sacram. iv. 4, 12: "The word of Christ maketh the sacrament."

[7] S. Greg. Illum. Armen. [30], quoted by Niceph. c. Euseb. in Spic. Solesm. p. 500.

" The Lord Jesus gives us the true Bread: He eateth with us, and Himself is eaten; we drink His Blood, and without Him we cannot drink It[1]." " His own Divine Flesh and His Precious Blood hath He given us to eat and to drink for the remission of sins[2]." " Our Lord has given us His own Flesh as food[3]." " His Blood becometh to believers a saving drink[4]." " A Body is ministered from Heaven[5]." " In place of all those sacrifices and oblations, His Body is offered and is ministered to Communicants[6]." They say that " the Communicant knoweth both the Flesh and Blood of the Word of God[7]." " When ye receive the Body of the Lord, ye guard It with all caution and veneration, lest ever so little of it fall, lest aught of the consecrated gift drop off[8]." " His Body is set before us now[9]." " The hand receives the Lord's Body[10]."

They reprove those who are defiled, if they " ap-

[1] S. Jerome, Ep. 120, ad Hedib. 9. 2.

[2] S. Hippol. [9] in Prov. 9, i. p. 282, ed. Fabr.

[3] S. James Nisib. Serm. xiv. § 6, p. 345.

[4] S. Greg. Nyss. de Vit. Mos. i. p. 244.

[5] Liberius [31] ap. S. Ambros. de Virg. iii. 1. 1.

[6] S. Aug. de Civ. Dei, xvii. 20, § 2.

[7] Orig. in Lev. Hom. 9, n. 10 : lit. " He who hath been initiated in the mysteries, knoweth " &c.

[8] Id. in Exod. Hom. 13, n. 3.

[9] S. Chrys. Hom. 51, in S. Matt. n. 3.

[10] S. Cypr. Ep. 58, ad Thibarit. § 10, p. 149, Oxf. Tr., and Inscript. Augustod. [8] in Spicil. Solesm. i. 557.

proach [1] their hands to," "invade [2]," "offend [3],"
"presume to touch [4]," "violate [5]," "offer violence
to [6]," "pollute [7]," "defile [8]," "profane [9]" the Body
of the Lord; "receive the Lord's Body in defiled
hands, and drink the Lord's Blood with polluted
mouth [10];" "insult the Blood of Christ [11];" "receive
with insolence the Body of Him who is God over
all [12];" "that Body, the spotless, the pure, the asso-
ciate with the Divine Nature." "How, think ye,"
they say, "is it less guilt to neglect the Word of
God than to neglect His Body [13]?"

They blame those through whom "before Jews
and Heathen an examination takes place as to the
Body and Blood of Christ [14]." They say that "in a
tumult the most Holy Blood of Christ was spilled [15];"

[1] Tertull. [7] de Idol. c. 7, p. 228, Oxf. Tr.

[2] S. Cypr. de Laps. § 11, p. 163, Oxf. Tr.

[3] Tertull. de Idol. l. c.

[4] S. Dionys. [12] Ep. ad Basil. can. 2. S. Firmil. [11] ap.
S. Cypr. Ep. 75, § 23, p. 282, Oxf. Tr.

[5] S. Pacian [38] Paraen. ad Paen. § 13, p. 370.

[6] S. Cypr. l. c.

[7] S. Jerom. in Mal. 1. 7, T. vi. p. 949, ed. Vall.

[8] S. Chrys. non esse ad grat. concion. § 1. ii. 659.

[9] S. Cypr. Ep. 15, ad Mart. § 1, p. 38, Oxf. Tr.

[10] S. Cypr. de Laps. § 14, p. 167, Oxf. Tr.

[11] S. Ath. Apol. c. Arian. § 11. See p. 30, Oxf. Tr.

[12] S. Chrys. in 1 Cor. Hom. 24, § 7, p. 333, Oxf. Tr.

[13] Orig. Hom. 13, in Exod. § 3, l. c.

[14] S. Julius [24] in S. Athan. Apol. ag. Arians, § 31, p. 52,
Oxf. Tr. The calumny was that Macarius had broken a chalice.
Ib. p. 28, 90, 9. 3.

[15] S. Chrys. Ep. i. ad Innocent. § 3, T. iii. p. 519.

" the soldiers scattered the Body and Blood of Christ on the pavement [1];" the Donatists " broke the Chalices, which bare the Blood of Christ [2];" they say, " our sanctuaries are now, as ever, pure, dignified by the Blood of Christ alone, and by piety towards Him [3]."

They speak of " having the senses purified, so as to be able to eat the living Bread and His life-giving Flesh, and to drink His saving Blood [4];" "preparing for the sanctifying of souls and bodies, that they may be able to endure the Blood and Body of the Lord, the Saviour [5];" " abstain," they say, " from all uncleanness, and then take the Body and Blood of Christ, and carefully guard thy mouth, by which the King has entered [6];" " be holy and spotless, and so eat the Body of Christ and drink the Blood of Christ [7];" " have no anger in thy heart, if thou desire to receive the Body of Christ [8];" " touch not the Body of Christ with a fevered hand [9]." Idola-

[1] Victor Vit. de Persecut. Vandal. L. i. B. P. viii. 678. (His date, A. 484, is later by some years than that of the writers here quoted.)

[2] S. Opt. [37] de Schism. Don. vi. 2, p. 92, ed. Du Pin.

[3] Ep. Synod. Alex. [25], in S. Ath. Apol. c. Arian, § 5, p. 20, Oxf. Tr. (against charge of blood-shedding).

[4] Euseb. in Ps. 36. 4, Montf. Nov. Coll. i. 149.

[5] S. Theodore (successor of S. Pachomius) [27], Epist. de Pasch. Gall. iv. 734.

[6] S. James Nis. Serm. 3, de Jejun. § 2, p. 46.

[7] S. Basil [40], Reg. 80, c. 22.

[8] Isaias Abb. [47], Reg. ad Mon. n. 50, Gall. vii. 323.

[9] S. Ambros. de Vid. c. 10, n. 65 ; ii. 203.

ters are " cut off from the Body and Blood of Christ,
whereby, long since, when re-born, they were re-
deemed [1]."

The Council of Nice says, "neither the rule nor
practice handed down that they who have not
power to offer should give the Body of Christ to
those who offer [2]." Other fathers say that " the
priests are entrusted with [3]," " minister [4]," " handle [5],"
" give [6]," " distribute the Body of Christ [7];" " give to
drink His Blood, the Cup of His Blood [8];" " present
the Body of Christ [9];" that " the priests approach to
the approaching God [10];" " the Deacons carry the
Body and Blood of Christ [11]." To them " is com-
mitted the consecrated Blood of Christ [12]." It is

[1] S. Siricius [53], Ep. i. ad Himer. c. 3, Conc. ii. 1214, ed. Col.

[2] Can. 18, Conc. ii. 42 [18].

[3] S. Basil, Ep. 53, Chorep. § 1. iii. 147.

[4] S. Ambros. l. c.

[5] S. Greg. Naz. [42], Or. 21, § 7, p. 389.

[6] S. Jerome, adv. Lucif. § 3 ; ii. 173, ed. Vall.

[7] S. Basil, Ep. 199 (Canon. 2), Can. 27 ; iii. 294.

[8] S. Ath. Apol. c. Arian. § 11.

[9] " Obtulit Sancto [Ambrosio] Christi Corpus." Paulin.
(Diac.) [68] Vit. S. Ambros. § 47, T. ii. App. p. xii.

[10] S. Greg. Naz. l. c.

[11] Philo Carpas. [63] in Cant. vii. 4, p. 164, ed. Rom.

[12] S. Laurence in S. Ambr. [14] de Off. i. 41, p. 214 : " Cui
commisisti Domini sanguinis consecrationem." I have rendered
' consecratio' as the abstract for the concrete. However deacons
may have, here and there, irregularly consecrated, this was always
regarded as a presumption. Carpentier (Supp. Du Cange v.
Consecratio) quotes the words in the Canon Missæ of the con-

enacted that, "when need be, they may deliver to the people the Eucharist of the Body of Christ[1]." They are bidden, "give not to the unworthy the purple of the sinless Body[2]."

Again, of that which we receive they say, "We eat Him[3];" "eat Him entire as Life[4];" "we eat life[5];" "receive the Bread of the Lord's Body[6];" "eat the Body and drink the Blood, if thou desire life[7]; "eat the Living Bread and the life-giving

secrated elements: " Hæc commixtio et consecratio Corporis et Sanguinis Domini," &c. The words used by S. Laurence are probably taken from that formula.

[1] Stat. Eccl. Ant., or Conc. Cart. iv. can. 38 [62], Conc. ii. 1440 [quoted Dist. 93, c. 18].

[2] S. Ath. in S. Matt. Montf. Nov. Coll. ii. p. 35.

[3] S. Ath. Exp. in Ps. 118, v. 171; i. 1219. S. Chrys. de Capt. Eutrop., § 8; iii. 393. Hom. 82, in S. Matt., § 4, p. 1091. O. T., &c.: "He feeds on the richness of the Lord's Body, the Eucharist," Tertull. de Pudic. c. 9, p. 725, D. ed. Rig. S. Ephrem Syr., Rh. 10, p. 148, Oxf. Tr. and not. h. Rh. 3. p. 22. R. 5, p. 32, not. 148 and not. h. S. Jerome, Ep. 21 ad Dam. 26, p. 79, ed. Vallar.

[4] S. Theoph. Al. [54] Fragm. ex Ep. Fest. i. ap. Cosm. in Montf. Nov. Coll. ii. 320.

[5] S. Jam. Nisib., Serm. 14, § 6, p. 347. S. Ambr. in Ps. 118, S. 18, § 28, p. 1203.

[6] S. Chromat. [65], Tract. 13, in St. Matt. § 5. Gall. viii. 348. Comp. S. Basil Mor. Reg. 21. Reg. 80, c. 22.

[7] S. Greg. Naz. Or. 45, § 19, p. 860. "He sent forth those two Baptisms from His pierced side, that those who had been washed with water might also drink His Blood." Tert. de Bapt. c. 16, p. 274, Oxf. Tr. Melito [4], explaining the Parable of Papias, interprets S. John vi. of the Holy Eucharist, Spicil. Solesm., Proleg. p. 6.

Flesh, and drink His saving Blood[1];" " the [2]Flesh of
Christ, which is indeed the Body of Life[2];" "that
true Bread, the Living Word[3];" " that everlasting
Word equal to the Father, wherewith Angels are
fed[4];" " Christ—the Body of God—the God of
Heaven[5];" " the Body of the Lord Jesus, in whom
is remission of sins[6];" the [7]Body of the Author (of
all things); " the Body of Him who hath life in
Himself (τῆς αὐτοζωῆς), who, for our sakes taber-
nacled in our body, who is Christ, the Son of the
Living God, one of the Holy Trinity[8];" "the
proper Body of Him who is by Nature life, the
Only-Begotten[9];" "a food whom whosoever neg-
lecteth to eat and drink, cannot have life in himself,
as the Lord Himself saith[10]." " We drink the Blood

[1] Eus. in Ps. 36, 4, p. 149, ed. Montf. S. Basil, Hom. in
S. Bapt., § 2, ii. 115.

[2] S. Ambrose de Myst., c. 8, § 48, ii. 337. " If we do not
eat the bread of life, if we do not eat the Flesh of Christ, and
are not made to drink of the Blood of Christ," &c., Orig. Hom.
18, in Luc. T. 3, p. 977.

[3] S. Macar. Hom. 47, n. 11.

[4] S. Aug. in Ps. 33, § 6, i. 346, Oxf. Tr.

[5] Salvian [76], adv. Avarit., L. ii. p. 247, ed. Bal.

[6] S. Ambr. in Ps. 118, S. 8, § 48, p. 1074.

[7] Id. de Myst., c. 8, fin.

[8] S. Cyril. Al. [66], Hom. in Myst. Cœn. T. v., P. ii.
p. 378.

[9] Id. Ep. in S. Symbol. T. v., P. 2, p. 189.

[10] S. Max. Taur. [69], Hom. 45, in P. 22 (quoting S.
John, 6).

of our redemption [1];" "we drink the Immortal Blood of Christ; our blood is joined to the Blood of Christ [2];" "life-giving Blood is offered to our lips [3];" "we drink His Holy Blood to the propitiation for our sins, and participation of the immortality in Him [4]." "The Church gives us daily that antidote of sorrow, the pure, true Blood of Christ [5];" "we receive the mystical Cup of the Blood of the Lord for the protection of our body and soul [6]." "We are fed from the Cross of the Lord, because we eat His Body [7];" "we drink not water from a rock, but Blood from His Side [8];" "we receive Him and lay Him up in ourselves, and place the Saviour in our breasts [9]." "He gives to thee the bread of blessing, His own Body, and bestows His own Blood [10];" "we partake of [11]," "receive

[1] S. Leo [75], Serm. 42 (de Quadr. iv.), c. 5, p. 161.

[2] Jul. Firm. [26] de Err. Prof. Relig., p. 44, ed. Ouz.

[3] Thecla and Martyrs under Sapor [28] (quoted Klee, Dogmatik, B. 2, p. 197).

[4] S. Cyr. in Myst. Cœn. l. c.

[5] S. Epiph. [36], Expos. Fid. Cath., p. 1096, 7.

[6] Hilar. Diac. [33] in 1 Cor. xi. 26. App. S. Ambr. ii. 149.

[7] S. Aug. in Ps. 100, n. 9. T. iv. p. 1088 [Ps. 101, iv. 491, Oxf. Tr.].

[8] S. Chrys. in Ps. 46, § 2, v. 189.

[9] S. Clem. Alex. [6], Pæd. i. 6, p. 123. S. Clement adds εἰ δυνατόν, "as far as possible," because we receive Him who, as God, is infinite.

[10] Orig. in Jerem. Hom. 18, § 13. iii. 256.

[11] Dionys. Ep. ad Xyst. [ap. Eus. H. E. vii. 9]. S. Pet. Alex. [16] can. 8 (Routh, Reliq. iv. 31). S. Cyril Jer. Cat.

His Body and Blood [1]," "that saving Body, Christ
Himself [2]." "Eating and drinking the Crucified [3],"
"on every Lord's Day we are quickened by the
hallowed Body of the same Saviour's Passover, and
are sealed in our souls by His precious Blood [4]."
"If we will, we have Him entire [5];" "we become
Christ-bearers, His Body and His Blood being dif-
fused through our members [6]." "The Christian,"
they say, "is fully convinced that he receives not
mere bread and wine, but truly the Body and Blood
of the Son of God, sanctified by the Holy Spirit [7]."
"Faith gave me the pen of the Spirit, and I took, I
wrote, and I confessed 'This is the Body of God [8].'"
"What we receive is the Body of Christ, and Christ
is Life [9]." "As He lives by the Father, so we live

Myst. iv. 3. S. Ath. de Incarn. c. Arian, n. 16, fin. p. 883.
S. Basil, Ep. 93, ad Cæsar. init. p. 186. Mor. Reg. 21. S.
Theoph. Al. Epist. Pasch. xi. S. Chrys. Hom. 2, ad Pop. Ant.
fin. (on the Statues, p. 53), de Bapt. Christi, § 4, p. 373, &c.

[1] Euseb. in Ps. 33, 9 (Montf. i. 132). S. Hil. de Trin. viii.
13. S. Ephr. in Exod. c. 12, T. 3, p. 213 (Select Works, p. 32,
n. ed. Oxf.).

[2] Is. Reg. ad Mon. Eus. in Ps. 21, 30. Montf. 1, 85, n. 50.

[3] S. Aug. in Ps. 33. Enarr. 2, § 10 (Ps. 34, p. 361, Oxf.
Tr.).

[4] Eus. de Pasch. Scriptt. Vett. Coll. Maii, i. p. 257.

[5] S. Chrys. in S. Matt., Hom. 51, § 3, p. 683, Oxf. Tr.

[6] S. Cyril Jerus. Cat. Myst. iv. 3, p. 271, Oxf. Tr.

[7] Jerome of Jerus. [55], Comm. util. Gall. vii. 529.

[8] S. Isaac the Great [57], Serm. de Fide in Ass. B. O. i.
220.

[9] Marius Victorin. [34] adv. Arian. ii. 8.

by His Flesh[1]." " He Himself is in us through the Flesh, and we are in Him[2]." " He mingles His Body in our body, and blends His Spirit with ours[3]." " In us there is a portion from Himself." " We receive Him within us that we may become the same as He[4]." " He commingleth Himself with us, and not by faith only, but in very deed maketh us His Body[5]." " That whereat Angels gaze with awe, thereby are we nourished; therewith are we mingled, and we become the one Body and the one Flesh of Christ." " He feeds us with His own Blood, and by every means entwines us with Himself[6]." " That same Flesh and Blood whereby He became akin to us, He gives forth to us. Wishing to show the longing He hath towards us, He hath mingled Himself with us, and blended His Body with ours, that we might in a manner be one thing, as the body joined to the Head[7]." " Christ gives us of His Flesh to be filled, drawing us on to greater love[8]." " He nourisheth and cherisheth the Church, and giveth her His own Body and Blood[9]." " That

---

[1] S. Hil. de Trin. viii. 16.

[2] Ib. § 14.

[3] S. Ephr. [39] Necros., Can. 12, T. vi. p. 246, ed. Ben. See also in " Select Works of S. Ephr." p. 346, note, ed. Oxf.

[4] S. Greg. Nyss., Hom. 8, in Eccl. T. i. p. 457.

[5] S. Chrys. in S. Matt., Hom. 82, § 5, p. 1091, Oxf. Tr.

[6] Ib. p. 1092.

[7] S. Chrys. in S. Joh. Hom. 46, § 3, p. 399, Oxf. Tr.

[8] Id. in 1 Cor. Hom. 24, § 7, fin. p. 334, Oxf. Tr.

[9] Theodoret in Ep. ad Eph. v. 29. iii. 434, ed. Sch.

very Body which sitteth above, is adored by Angels,
is nigh to the Power incorruptible, of this do we
taste[1]." "Whensoever we approach to His Body
and Blood, and take It on our hands, so we embrace
His Body, and are made (as it is written) of His
Flesh and of His Bones[2]." "Thou who receivest
the Flesh, partakest, in that Food, of His Divine
substance[3]." "We are called Christ's Body and
members, as receiving through the Eucharist the
Son Himself within us[4]." "That deathless Body
coming to be in him who receives It, transmutes our
whole being into Its own Nature[5]." "The precious
and undefiled Body and Blood of Christ, the God of
all, purify from every defilement those who partake
thereof with much fear and earnestness[6]." "Christ
cometh to be in us through His own Flesh[7]." "Those
who are in Christ He Himself sanctifies, holily offered
through the mystical Eucharist, wherein we are
blessed and quickened[8]." "He gives Himself for a

[1] S. Chrys. in Ep. ad Eph. Hom. 3, § 3. See p. 130, Oxf. Tr.

[2] S. Maruthas [59], Comm. in Evang. ap. Assem. B. O. i.
180.

[3] Auct. de Sacr. [51], vi. 1, ap. S. Ambr. ii. 381.

[4] S. Cyril Al. in S. Joh. vi. 56 fin. L. iv. p. 364.

[5] S. Greg. Nyss. Orat. Catechet., according to Maii's text,
Nov. Coll. vi. 368.

[6] S. Nilus [77], Ep. i. 44, ad Philipp. Schol., p. 21, ed.
Rom.

[7] S. Hil. de Trin. viii. 1. S. Cyril (in S. Joh. vi. 55), L. iv.
p. 363, and again, p. 365.

[8] Tit. Bostr. [35] in Luk. 22, 4, in Cramer, Catena ii. 155.

spiritual feast and banquet [1]." "He has given us to
be filled with His holy Flesh. He has set before
us Himself sacrificed [2]." "He who gave Himself as
the Bread of life, Who poured out His Blood into
the Cup of salvation [3]." "He who receiveth the
Flesh of our Saviour Christ, and drinketh His
Precious Blood, as He saith, is found as one thing
with Him, commingled, as it were, and immingled
with Him through the participation, so that he is
found in Christ, and Christ again in him [4]." "The
Body [of Christ] is not Consubstantial with the
Word from God, yet is one by that ineffable coming-
together and concurrence ; and since the Flesh of
the Saviour became life-giving, as being united to
That which is, by nature, Life, the Word from God,
then, when we taste It, we have life in ourselves,
we too being united with It, as It to the in-
dwelling Word." "The [5] Holy Body of Christ
giveth life to those in whom It is, and holdeth

---

[1] S. Chrys. in S. Matt. 8, 4. Hom. 25, § 5, p. 383, Oxf.
Tr.

[2] Id. in S. Matt. 14, 36. Hom. 50, § 3, p. 684.

[3] S. Pet. Chrysol. [72], Serm. 2, de prodig. fil. B. P. vii.
847.

[4] S. Cyr. in S. Joh. 6, 57. L. iv. p. 365.—The same language
is ascribed to Victor of Antioch [64], in Cramer's Cat. in Marc.
14, 24, p. 423, and Apollinarius [45] in S. Joh. vi. 52 (Cramer,
T. 2, p. 255). "This that He said, ' He that eateth My Flesh,
and drinketh My Blood, abideth in Me and I in Him,' showed
that He is immingled (ἀνακιρνᾶται) in him."

[5] Id. in S. Joh. 6, 35, L. iii. c. 6, p. 324.

them together in incorruption, being mingled (ἀνακιρ-νάμενον) with our bodies. For we know it to be the Body of none other than of Him Who is, by Nature, Life, having in itself the whole virtue of the united Word, and qualitied, as it were (πεποιωμέ-νον), yea, rather filled with His mighty working, whereby all things are made alive, and kept in being." " The participation of the Body and Blood of Christ effects nothing else, than that we pass into that we receive [1]." " Not even by 'the mouth of babes' is the truth of the Body and Blood of Christ, among the Sacraments of Communion, unconfessed. For in that mystic distribution of spiritual nourishment this is imparted, this received ; that we, receiving the virtue of the heavenly Food, may pass into the Flesh of Himself who was made our Flesh [2]."

To close this list with an encyclical letter of S. Cyril, adopted by the General Council of Ephesus, " We approach to the Eucharist and are sanctified, having partaken of the Holy Flesh, and the precious Blood of Christ, the Saviour of us all ; and receiving it not as common flesh, God forbid ! but as truly life-giving, and the own Flesh of the Word Himself. For He, as God, being by nature, Life, when He became one with His Flesh, made it life-giving. So that though He say to us, ' Verily, verily, I say unto you, except ye eat the Flesh of the Son of Man, and drink His Blood,' we shall not account it as the

[1] S. Leo [61], Serm. 63 [de Pass. 12], fin. p. 247.
[2] Id. Ep. 59, ad cler. et pleb. Const. c. 2, p. 977.

E

flesh of one of us ; (for how shall the Flesh of a man be, by its own nature, life-giving ?) but as having become truly the own Flesh of Him, Who, for us, became, and was called, the Son of Man [1]."

The prayers of the ancient Church agree with and express her teaching [2]. "The rule of prayer forms the rule of faith. The transmitted prayers of the Church hold in life and being, her transmitted faith." The ancient Liturgies, wherein they agree [3], express one origin of the Christian worship throughout the world ; and that origin, in its substance, from the Apostles, and so from God. Yet in every way they do, with one harmony of prayer (whether for the Gift itself, or that the soul may be made meet for that gift), of confession, of belief, or of thanksgiving, express the doctrine of the real Presence of the Body and Blood of Christ. They pray that " the [4] Holy Spirit would

[1] S. Cyril et Synod. Alex. ad Nestor. c. 7, in Conc. Eph. P. 1, c. 26. Conc. T. iii. p. 951, ed. Col. (quoted Decr. de Consecr. D. 2, c. 80.)

[2] "Ut legem credendi lex statuat supplicandi." Cælest. 1, Ep. 1, ad Episc. Gall. Conc. iii. 475.

[3] See the arguments drawn out in Tracts for the Times, No. 63, on the Antiquity of the existing Liturgies ; and in Archdn. Wilberforce, "Doctrine of the Holy Eucharist," c. 3.

[4] S. Cyril Jerus. Cat. Myst. v. 7, p. 275, Oxf. Tr. Lit. S. Jacob. (Assem. Cod. Lit. v. 40.) S. Marc. (Assem. vii. 35.) S. Basil (Ib. 59, 60). S. Gregory (Ib. p. 106, 7). S. Chrysostom. ($\lambda\epsilon\iota\tau o\upsilon\rho\gamma$. a, p. $\nu\eta$, β. p. $\mu\gamma$, γ. p. ξa. ed. Ven. 1644.) S. Cyril (p. 183). The Roman Canon has a corresponding prayer before the consecration, "Quem oblationem Tu, Deus, in

make this Bread the Body, and this Cup the Blood
of the New Testament of our Lord God and Saviour and Sovereign King, Jesus Christ." Or they
confess, " the Holy Body, and precious, very, Blood
of Jesus Christ, Son of God, Amen. The Holy,
Precious Body and very Blood of Jesus Christ, the
Son of God, Amen. I believe, I believe, I believe, and
confess to my last breath, that this is the life-giving
Flesh of Thy Only-Begotten Son, our Lord and God,
and Saviour Jesus Christ, Amen[1]." Or for themselves they pray that they " may without condemnation partake of the Holy Body and Precious Blood
for the remission of sin and life eternal[2]." In
thanksgiving they pray that " the Communion of the
Holy Body and Precious Blood of the Only-Begotten
Son may be to faith unashamed, love unfeigned,
fulness of holiness, repulse of the adversary, fulfil-
ment of the Commandment, provision by the way to
life eternal, an acceptable defence at the fearful
judgment-seat of Jesus Christ[3];" or "that we who

omnibus benedictam, ascriptam, ratam, rationabilem, acceptabi-
lemque facere digneris, ut nobis Corpus et Sanguis fiat dilec-
tissimi Fili tui Domini Dei nostri J. C.," which the Author of the
de Sacram. (iv. 5. 21, ap. S. Ambr. ii. 371) includes in the
formula of Consecration. Add Mabillon, Miss. Franc. p. 327,
and also Miss. Goth. 202. 208. 228. 301. Mone Missen, p. 19.
21, 22. Sacram. Leon. Opp. S. Leon. T. ii. p. 150, ed. Baller.

[1] Lit. S. Basil, Assem. vii. 77, 78. S. Gregory, Ib. p. 128.

[2] Lit. S. James, Ass. v. 57.

[3] Lit. of S. Mark, Ass. vii. p. 41, 42 (a prayer adopted by
Bp. Andrewes); add. Lit. of St. James, Ass. v. 59.

have[1] spiritually received the most Holy Body of our Lord Jesus Christ, being stripped of carnal sins, may attain to be made spiritual[2]."

Christ redeems us not, my younger brethren, to part with us. He cometh not to us, to part from us; He cometh to abide with us, if we will have Him. He will come to us in holiness, righteousness, sanctification, redemption, if we will long for Him,—if in faith and charity we will receive Him. He will cleanse your dross, slake your feverishness, chase away foul thoughts, re-create your decay, drive off Satan, gather you up into Himself. He will strengthen you against temptation, lift you up above those miserable, maddening, seducing pleasures of sense, and give you a foretaste of heavenly sweetness, of blissful calm, of spiritual joy, of transporting love, of unearthly delight, in His own ever-blessed, ever-blessing, Presence. Martyrs of old went to their last conflict "fortified," S. Cyprian[3] says, "with the protection of the Body and Blood of Christ." By His Body and Blood will Christ prepare *you* for

[1] Mabillon, Missal. Goth. p. 192 (Post Communion); add Ib. p. 190. 293. 297. 300; Miss. Gall. Vet. p. 331. 347.

[2] This paragraph upon the liturgies, as well as many of the preceding extracts from the Fathers, were omitted in preaching, for want of time; but those passages were delivered which presented the same truth in a variety of ways, and no way of expressing the doctrine was omitted.

[3] Council under S. Cyprian to Cornel. Ep. 56, § 1, p. 138, Oxf. Tr.

your conflict. Satan stands in awe of you. "If they," says S. Chrysostom, "who touched the hem of His garment, drew from Him such great virtue, how much more they who possess Him wholly[1]?" "Ask," he says, "even the devil himself, whence hast thou that incurable wound? whence hast thou no longer any strength? whence art thou captive? wherewith wert thou taken in thy flight? Nought else will he say than this, The Body which was crucified[2]!" "As to approach carelessly is peril, so not to partake of that mystical Feast is famine and death. For this Table is the nerve of our soul, the band of our thought, the foundation of our confidence, our hope, our salvation, our light, our life[3]."

Christ dwells in us in a twofold way, spiritually and sacramentally. By His Spirit, He makes us the temples of God; by His Body and Blood, He is to our bodies also a source of life, incorruption, immortality. "Ye are the temples of the Holy Ghost." As you would reverence the Church of God, so and much more reverence yourselves as His Temples. As you would reverence the Holy Sepulchre, so and yet more reverence yourselves, your own bodies, which, our Church says, have been "made clean by His Body, and washed with His most Precious Blood." Reverence, beforehand, your souls and bodies. If ye believe Christ and His Word, ye know that, when ye do come to the Holy Eucharist,

---

[1] In S. Matt. Hom. 50, § 3, p. 683, Oxf. Tr.

[2] Id. in 1 Cor. x. 24, Hom. 24, n. 7, p. 333, O. T.

[3] Ib. § 8, p. 335.

ye come to the Communion of the Body and Blood of Christ. Were He Himself visibly present, and ye to come into His Presence, ye would not, just before ye came into His Presence, defile your imaginations, or, whether men know of it or no (ye whom it concerns, know what I mean), first fever your own frames, and then, in a way which Christ forbids and hates, remove that feverishness.

"These things thou doest," says S. Chrysostom[1], " when thou hast enjoyed the Table of Christ, on that day on which thou hast been counted worthy to touch His Flesh with thy tongue. Whosoever thou art then, that those things be not so, do thou purify thy right hand, thy tongue, thy lips, which have become a threshold for Christ to tread on. I beseech you that we do not this to condemnation. Let us nourish Christ; let us give Him to drink; let us clothe Him. These things are worthy of that Table. Hast thou heard holy hymns? Hast thou seen a spiritual marriage? Hast thou enjoyed a royal Table? Hast thou been filled with the Holy Ghost? Hast thou joined in the quire of the Seraphim? Hast thou become partaker of the power above? Cast not away so great a joy; waste not the treasure; bring not in drunkenness, the mother of dejection, the joy of the devil, the parent of countless evils."

How can ye pray Him " to whom all hearts are open," to cleanse your thoughts by the inspiration of His Holy Spirit, and then admit into your souls, the

[1] Ib. Hom. 27, n. 7, p. 381, O. T.

very dwelling-place of God, thoughts hateful to God, and, when ye come to yourselves, to yourselves also? He has made you, He says, "members" of Himself, "of His Flesh, and of His Bones." He comes to dwell in you. Ye will not then utter, with lips which belong to Christ, words of profaneness, or of refined or coarse indecency, which ye would be shocked to utter in your parent's presence. Ye will not use the Word of God for display of some poor but profane cleverness. Ye will not corrupt others, nor add to the corruption of those for whom, with you, Christ died. Ye are not your own; ye are joined to Christ; ye will not profane what is not yours, but Christ's.

Past sin excludes no penitent sinner from any nearness to Christ. Present weakness or sickness hinders none from coming to the Physician of Life. We come to the Physician, not because we are whole, but because we are sick. But ye must not come to this immediate Presence of Christ, the Church tells you, without "true repentance for past sins, and a stedfast purpose to lead a new life." Ye must not return "from the sky to the sty[1]." To what end to pretend again and again to desire that the soul should be washed in Christ's precious Blood, and then ever anew to return to the "wallowing in the mire?" To what end, against God's Word, first to "drink the Cup of the Lord," and then "the Cup of devils?" And what else is it than to drink the

---

[1] "A cœlo ad cœnum." Tert. de Spect. § 25, p. 214, O. T.

Cup of devils, to be giddy with the fumes of passion, to be out of yourselves, to lose control over yourselves, to do in feverish haste what God forbids, what defiles yourselves, what ye are forthwith ashamed of, and hate, and would gnash with your teeth that ye had done?

And what are ye yourselves, my brethren, who do these things? What are ye wasting in yourselves? God, the Word, became Flesh, to redeem you. He, the Only-Begotten Son of God, for you made Man, giveth Himself to you to dwell in you, and make you one with Him. This He does for you in time, while you are yet in this clay, absent from Him, seeing Him not, save by the eye of faith; touching Him with the hands of the heart, and if ye will, ye, by that inner touch, " taste and see that the Lord is gracious." What must be your value in the sight of God, that for you God the Father should have given His Only-Begotten Son; for you, Christ, God and man, died! You He would knit as closely to Himself, as the food of the body is united with the body. If such be the earnest, what will be the fulness? If such are the rays of His love, seen through a glass darkly, what when we see " face to face?" If such be the closeness of union when you are absent from the Lord, what when ye are " present" and " dissolved, and are with Christ?" If this be the gift of His goodness to you in " this body of death," when "the corruptible body presseth down the soul," what when your body too shall be spiritual,

conformed to His glorious Body, which is glorious
with the Glory of the Father, the In-dwelling Godhead, Light Unapproachable!

"The Holy Eucharist is," the Homilies[1] say, "the
salve of immortality and sovereign preservative
against death, a deifical Communion, the sweet dain-
ties of our Saviour, the pledge of eternal health, the
defence of faith, the hope of the resurrection, the
food of immortality, the healthful grace, and the
conservatory to everlasting life." It has then a
heavenly sweetness, the foretaste of the eternal,
against the destructive sweetness of this world's
pleasures. It has sweetness because Christ is sweet
to the soul; it is "healthful grace," because Christ
is our health, and the Author of Grace; it is the
"defence of faith," because Christ is "the Author
and Finisher of our faith;" it is "the Food of immortality, and the hope of the Resurrection, the
pledge of eternal health, and the sovereign preservative against death," because Christ is all these, and
all besides; "our Redemption and Salvation," "the
Resurrection and the Life."

Wait but a little, pray your Redeemer for endurance, and all ye long for ye shall have, not against
the will of God, but from His Love, and the fulness
of His Good Pleasure. Then for these feverish
pleasures, ye shall be filled and overflowed with the
torrent of His pleasure; then, for maddening joys,

---

[1] Second Part of the Sermon upon the Sacraments.

F

ye shall enter into, be immersed in, the joy of your own Lord. Then shall your soul be irradiated with the light of Divine Wisdom, your mind be enlightened with Divine knowledge, your body be clothed with the glory of God, wherewith ye shall be encompassed. Then shall ye gaze unceasingly on Beauty which eye hath not seen,—the Face of God. The Brightness of His Glory, and the Infinity of His Love, and the Unchangeableness of His joy, and the hidden treasures of His Knowledge, and His Incomprehensible Essence, shall be in your measure apprehended by you. Then shall all truth be open to you, all love shall fill you; soul and body shall be satisfied with His likeness; they shall rest in His love; they shall have all they long for, and long for all they have. All you long for, shall be for ever yours; for the All Holy Trinity shall be for ever yours; the glorified Humanity of your Lord shall be for ever yours; and meanwhile, if you pray Him to cleanse His dwelling-place, your soul, He will cleanse it. He will empty it of what is not His; He will fill it with what is His; He will fill it with His Grace, fill you with Himself, the Author of Grace, as He saith, "If a man love Me, he will keep My saying, and My Father will love him, and We will come unto him, and make our abode in him." Amen.

GILBERT AND RIVINGTON, PRINTERS, ST. JOHN'S SQUARE, LONDON.

WORKS

REV. E. B. PUSEY, D.D.

The CHURCH the CONVERTER of the HEATHEN. Two Sermons, 1838 ; with copious Notes. 12mo. Third Edition. 6d.

CHRIST the SOURCE and RULE of CHRISTIAN LOVE. With a Preface on the Relation of our Exertions to our Needs. 1s. 6d.

The PREACHING of the GOSPEL a Preparation for our Lord's Coming. 1841. 1s.

GOD is LOVE. Whoso receiveth one such Little Child in My Name, receiveth Me. Two Sermons. 1846. 1s. 6d.

The DAY of JUDGMENT. 1839. Second Edition. 6d.

The HOLY EUCHARIST: a Comfort for the Penitent. 1843. 1s. 6d.

ENTIRE ABSOLUTION of the PENITENT. 1846. Two Sermons. 1s. 6d. and 1s.

CHASTISEMENTS NEGLECTED, Forerunners of Greater. On the General Fast Day, 1847. 1s.

The BLASPHEMY against the HOLY GHOST. 1845. 1s.

ELEVEN SERMONS preached at the Consecration of St. Saviour's, Leeds, 1845. Together with Sermons by the Rev. J. KEBLE, Rev. Is. WILLIAMS, Rev. W. DODSWORTH, Rev. C. MARRIOTT, Rev. W. U. RICHARDS. 7s. 6d.

The ROYAL SUPREMACY not an Arbitrary Authority, but limited by the Laws of the Church of which Kings are Members. Part I. Ancient Precedents. 8vo, 7s. Part II. *In the Press.*

The CHURCH of ENGLAND leaves her CHILDREN FREE to whom to OPEN their GRIEFS. A Letter to the Rev. W. U. RICHARDS, Minister of Margaret Chapel. 8vo, 5s., or with Postscript, 8s. 6d.

The DANGER of RICHES. Seek God first, and ye shall have all. Two Sermons preached in the Parish Church of St. James's, Bristol. Published by request. 8vo, 1s. 6d.

The RULE of FAITH, as maintained by the Fathers and Church of England. A Sermon preached before the University, on the fifth Sunday after Epiphany, 1851. 8vo, 1s. 6d.

WORKS BY THE REV. E. B. PUSEY, D.D.

LETTER to the LORD BISHOP of LONDON, in Explanation of some Statements contained in a Letter by the Rev. W. DODSWORTH. 16mo, 1s.

RENEWED EXPLANATIONS in consequence of Mr. DODSWORTH's Comments on the above. 8vo, 1s.

PAROCHIAL SERMONS from ADVENT to WHITSUNTIDE. Vol. I. Third Edition. 8vo, cloth, 10s. 6d.

Devotional Works, adapted to the Use of the English Church.

FROM THE WORKS OF FOREIGN DIVINES.

EDITED BY THE REV. E. B. PUSEY, D.D.

The SPIRITUAL COMBAT, with the PATH of PARADISE; and the SUPPLEMENT; or, the Peace of the Soul. By SCUPOLI. (From the Italian.) Third edition, revised. With Frontispiece. 3s. 6d.

The YEAR of AFFECTIONS; or, Sentiments on the Love of God, drawn from the Canticles, for every Day in the Year. By AVRILLON. 6s. 6d.

The FOUNDATIONS of the SPIRITUAL LIFE. (A Commentary on Thomas à Kempis.) By SURIN. 4s. 6d.

The LIFE of JESUS CHRIST in GLORY. Daily Meditations from Easter Day to the Wednesday after Trinity Sunday. By NOUET. 8s. Or in Two Parts, at 4s. each.

PARADISE for the CHRISTIAN SOUL. By HORST. Two Vols., 6s. 6d. Or in Six Parts, at 1s. each.

DEVOTIONS for HOLY COMMUNION. 18mo, 1s.

LITANIES for PENITENTS. In the Words of Holy Scripture. Royal 32mo, 6d.

Uniform with the above.

FAMILIAR INSTRUCTIONS on MENTAL PRAYER. From the French of COURBON. With a Preface by the Editor. Part I. Price 6d.

J. H. PARKER, OXFORD, AND 377, STRAND, LONDON.